Art Weinstein, PhD

Handbook of Market Segmentation
Strategic Targeting for Business and Technology Firms

Third Edition

Pre-publication
REVIEWS,
COMMENTARIES,
EVALUATIONS . . .

"**M**ost businesses fail to segment their markets with any precision. Their profits could be much greater if they better defined their segments and aligned their offerings with their chosen segments. Art Weinstein has prepared a handbook for business and technology marketers that is rich in segmentation theory and case examples."

Philip Kotler, PhD
S. C. Johnson Professor of International Marketing,
Kellogg School of Management,
Northwestern University

"**T**he third edition of *Handbook of Market Segmentation* is a complete and fresh look at the notion of segmentation marketing. It is a practical guide for today's high-tech businessperson. As an international market analyst and a graduate school professor of international business, I have been using much of the material in the numerous new case studies both as a practitioner in the aviation industry and to supplement my lectures in the areas of strategic marketing planning and international business development."

Jude E. Edwards, DIBA
Market Analyst and Adjunct Professor
Capitol College of Engineering

More pre-publication
REVIEWS, COMMENTARIES, EVALUATIONS . . .

"**A**rt Weinstein explains in his insightful *Handbook of Market Segmentation* how to manage business segmentation and improve an enterprise's market performance by creating a segmentation-driven organization. This book contains valuable segmentation strategy cases of successful business and technology firms, useful tables and figures, and segmentation skillbuilders that make it easy for the reader to adapt the concrete advice into actual business strategies. This outstanding, comprehensive handbook offers examples to help the reader implement segmentation and targeting strategies based on a customer-driven focus."

Wolfgang Ridl, PhD
Head, Global Marketing Development,
Sandoz GmbH, Austria

—⚬⚬⚬—

"**M**ost businesses manage to determine target market priorities and to develop brand positionings with varying levels of professionalism. Many or-

ganizations never achieve segmentation. This insightful book properly explores how and why to segment.

The many practical insights offered throughout the *Handbook of Market Segmentation* demonstrate the author's unrivaled expertise in this area—as an academic and also as a consultant assisting marketing practitioners. This blend of experiences results in an awareness of the many pitfalls that businesses face as they endeavor to segment their markets.

The solutions to these impediments are presented in this well-constructed book. Cleverly conceived exercises in each chapter further demystify the common problems encountered during segmentation. The emphasis on 'how to' processes and tips is the real highlight of this excellent book. As well as being an essential resource for marketing students, this book offers vital and actionable guidance to marketing practitioners. The *Handbook of Market Segmentation* should be part of any marketer's book stock."

Sally Dibb, PhD
Lyndon Simkin, PhD
Readers in Marketing,
Warwick Business School,
University of Warwick, United Kingdom

The Haworth Press®
New York • London • Oxford

Handbook of Market Segmentation

Strategic Targeting for Business and Technology Firms

Third Edition

THE HAWORTH PRESS
Haworth Series in Segmented, Targeted, and Customized Marketing: Conceptual and Empirical Development
Art Weinstein

Handbook of Market Segmentation: Strategic Targeting for Business and Technology Firms, Third Edition by Art Weinstein

Other titles of related interest:

Marketing Management: Text and Cases by David Loudon, Robert Stevens, and Bruce Wrenn

Fundamentals of Business Marketing Research by David A. Reid and Richard E. Plank

Fundamentals of Business Marketing Education: A Guide for University-Level Faculty and Policymakers by J. David Lichtenthal

Strategic Global Marketing: Issues and Trends edited by Erdener Kaynak

Marketing Your Business: A Guide to Developing a Strategic Marketing Plan by Ronald A. Nykiel

Customer Advisory Boards: A Strategic Tool for Customer Relationship Building by Tony Carter

Social Marketing edited by Michael T. Ewing

Global Marketing Co-Operation and Networks edited by Leo Paul Dana

Cross-National Consumer Psychographics edited by Lynn R. Kahle

Newer Insights into Marketing: Cross-Cultural and Cross-National Perspective edited by Camille P. Schuster and Phil Harris

How Consumers Pick a Hotel: Strategic Segmentation and Target Marketing by Dennis J. Cahill

Geography and Tourism Marketing edited by Martin Oppermann

Handbook of Cross-Cultural Marketing by Paul A. Herbig

Marketing Planning Guide, Second Edition by Robert E. Stevens, Bruce Wrenn, David L. Loudon, and William E. Warren

The Marketing Research Guide by Robert E. Stevens, Bruce Wrenn, Morris E. Ruddick, and Philip K. Sherwood

Marketing Research That Pays Off: Case Histories of Marketing Research Leading to Success in the Marketplace edited by Larry Percy

Handbook of Market Segmentation
Strategic Targeting for Business and Technology Firms

Third Edition

Art Weinstein, PhD

The Haworth Press®
New York • London • Oxford

The Haworth Press, Inc., 10 Alice Street, Binghamton, NY 13904-1580.

An earlier edition of the book was published as *Market Segmentation: Using Demographics, Psychographics, and Other Niche Marketing Techniques to Predict Customer Behavior,* Revised Edition (Chicago, IL: Probus Publishing Co., 1994).

Cover design by Lora Wiggins.

Library of Congress Cataloging-in-Publication Data

Weinstein, Art.
     Handbook of market segmentation : strategic targeting for business and technology firms / Art Weinstein.—3rd ed.
          p. cm.
     Includes bibliographical references and index.
     ISBN 0-7890-2156-0 (alk. paper)—ISBN 0-7890-2157-9 (soft : alk. paper)
     1. Market segmentation. 2. Psychographics. I. Title.

HF5415.127.W45 2004
658.8'02—dc22

                                                                                              2003023392

To Sandee and Trevor, with love

ABOUT THE AUTHOR

Art Weinstein, PhD, is Professor and Chair of Marketing in the H. Wayne Huizenga School of Business and Entrepreneurship at Nova Southeastern University in Fort Lauderdale, Florida. He teaches graduate courses in customer value, international marketing, managerial marketing and research, and market segmentation.

Dr. Weinstein is a nationally known expert in segmentation and market definition. He has provided consulting and training services for Bayer Diagnostics, Hewlett-Packard, Intel, J&J/Cordis, Motorola, Novartis, and many companies, government agencies, professional associations, and universities.

Dr. Weinstein is the author of *Defining Your Market: Winning Strategies for High-Tech, Industrial, and Service Firms* (Haworth) and co-author of *Superior Customer Value in the New Economy: Concepts and Cases,* Second Edition. He was the founding editor of the *Journal of Segmentation in Marketing: Innovations in Market Identification and Targeting* and has written more than fifty articles and papers on marketing strategy issues. He is a member of the American Marketing Association and of the Academy of Marketing Science.

CONTENTS

PART IV: SEGMENTATION STRATEGY CASES

Preface

This book was written to provide marketing/business practitioners and scholars (professors and students) with an informative, state-of-the-art guide to strategically segmenting high-tech and industrial markets. While top executives often advocate being market/customer oriented, I have found that few companies use target marketing to its fullest potential. In spite of the many advances made in segmentation methodology and technology, a majority of firms base their marketing plans on cursory, incomplete, or intuitive analyses of their potential markets. However, used effectively, segmentation techniques are valuable for increasing sales and improving overall marketing performance.

Does your company suffer from the following marketing deficiencies?

- "Fuzzy" business mission
- Unclear objectives
- Information that is not decision oriented
- Lack of agreement as to segmentation's role in the firm
- Production-driven focus (products reflect corporate desires rather than customer needs)
- Unfocused promotional strategy
- Failure to attack niche markets

If you answered "yes" to any of these, you are not alone. Cognizant of such problems that are faced by successful Fortune 500 companies as well as most other companies, this book develops a systematic process for introducing and improving business segmentation planning and execution in your firm.

How important is segmentation to business marketers? Let us consider what two leading research sources stated. Based on input from over 100 leading marketing practitioners, an intensive competency model was developed by Allen Stines in cooperation with the Institute for the Study of Business Markets (ISBM) at Pennsylvania State University to define exceptional business-to-business (B2B) marketing management practices for the year 2007. Segmentation was operationalized as the technical manifestation of truly understanding the customer. It was rated the top B2B competency out of a pool of 153 marketing issues. According to Stines, superior performing companies use innovative market segmentation criteria and processes to find customers with similar needs and behaviors.[1]

According to the Marketing Science Institute (MSI), customer issues are first-tier research priorities for the years 2002 through 2004. Managing customers (a retention challenge) and understanding customers (anticipating needs) ranked third and fifth, respectively, of sixteen sets of marketing topics most in need of research. Viewed collectively, understanding and managing customers was the current number one priority of marketing managers and has placed in the top five over the ten-year period 1994 to 2004 (the other long-term priorities were metrics, growth and new products, brands, and marketing information/knowledge).[2]

If you are a marketer, manager/executive, or entrepreneur, you will find *Handbook of Market Segmentation: Strategic Targeting for Business and Technology Firms* (Third Edition) to be a valuable resource to assist you in segmenting markets. It is also a thought-provoking readings and casebook for advanced/graduate marketing students who want to go beyond theory and learn how to make "real world" strategy decisions in changing and competitive business markets.

Unlike the two prior editions of this book that addressed consumer and business segmentation, this edition has been completely revamped to focus solely on the unique segmentation challenges of business and technology markets. The vast majority of the 17,000-plus buyers of the earlier editions were business marketers (consistent with the Pareto principle, this is estimated at about 80 percent). Furthermore, most of my segmentation consulting and training engagements during the past decade were with high-tech, industrial, or business service organizations. Many of these relevant segmentation experiences are incorporated into this new edition.

Realizing your need for practical information, a highly theoretical and quantitative approach has been avoided. Instead, this book is a "how-to" guide to the effective use of market segmentation planning, techniques, and strategies in business markets. *Handbook of Market Segmentation* is built on the latest thinking from the business and academic communities. Much of the material appearing in this book has been discussed at length in master's (MBA) and doctoral courses and in executive seminars or is based on important research in leading marketing publications.

Business practitioners can readily apply these valuable market segmentation tools. By learning how other companies in your industry or related industries define and select markets, you are able to adapt the best practices and incorporate them into your planning, research, and strategy formation. The book is designed to help you put business segmentation concepts to immediate and profitable use.

In addition to many useful figures and tables, each chapter features a Business Segmentation Insight (an in-depth look at a key segmentation topic supported by research or practice) and a Segmentation Skillbuilder (field-tested exercises to help you improve your working knowledge of crucial B2B segmentation issues). Chapter notes direct readers to additional published work on areas of further interest.

Handbook of Market Segmentation is organized into four major parts for clarity and to facilitate rapid comprehension of the material presented:

> *Part I: Segmentation Planning* (Chapters 1, 2, and 3) provides a blueprint for conducting effective, cost-efficient, and profitable segmentation studies in business markets. An overview of market segmentation and niche marketing, market definition, and how to design segmentation studies and use segmentation research are discussed.

Part II: Business Segmentation Bases (Chapters 4, 5, 6, and 7) details the major business segmentation dimensions—i.e., geographics, firmographics, usage, benefits, purchasing behavior, organizational psychographics, and buyer adopter categories. In addition, significant coverage of the new North American Industrial Classification System (NAICS), business census products, and an important model for segmenting industrial markets (the nested approach) are featured.

Part III: Implementing Segmentation Strategy (Chapters 8 and 9) discusses target marketing, segment attractiveness, positioning, marketing strategy formulation in business markets, building a segmentation-driven organization, implementation issues, segmentation audits, and business segmentation challenges.

Part IV: Segmentation Strategy Cases presents six all-new, indepth examples of business segmentation approaches and strategies by a diverse group of organizations in highly competitive markets. The focal companies are Collins Aviation Services, Dev-Soft, Dow Corning, Lexmark International, Pharmacia Corporation, and Sportmed. These hands-on case studies also include end-of-case questions for analysis and suggestions for further reading.

Based on more than fifteen years of interesting and intriguing work in market segmentation research and strategy, I am convinced that market leadership is dependent upon how successful firms are at defining and selecting markets appropriate to their capabilities, resources, and competitive situation. I am pleased to share with you my blueprint and thoughts on how to improve an organization's marketing performance in new or existing business markets. Enjoy the educational experience. I look forward to learning more about your market segmentation trials, tribulations, and triumphs. Feel free to contact me at <art@huizenga.nova.edu>, (954) 262-5097 (phone), or (954) 441-2447 (fax), or visit my Web site at <http://home.bellsouth.net/p/PWP-artweinstein>.

Acknowledgments

Many individuals provided valuable input toward the preparation of the *Handbook of Market Segmentation,* Third Edition. First and foremost, I thank Bill Cohen, Bill Palmer, and the outstanding management team and staff at The Haworth Press for developing the Segmentation in Marketing book series. (Haworth really knows how to define and segment its market.) I am also indebted to J. Michael Jeffers for making the first two editions of the book possible.

Second, I thank my Nova Southeastern University colleagues. Randy Pohlman, Dean, and Preston Jones, Associate Dean, of the Huizenga School, as well as Ron Chenail, Assistant to the President for Academic Affairs, and President Ray Ferrero Jr. supported my 2003 faculty sabbatical that enabled me to research and write the book. Professor Bill Johnson discovered the Dow Corning case and assisted with some examples. Barbara Ireland and Sylvia Lanski word processed several cases and provided computer graphics for some key figures. Dean Vellenga, Reference Librarian, was helpful in the preparation of a table on secondary research sources. In addition, our MBA and doctoral students (particularly in my six-day seminar on market segmentation) provided an outstanding learning environment for refining this marketing body of knowledge.

Third, I must acknowledge the following individuals for their case studies, illustrative examples, and segmentation insights in the book. In alphabetical order, thank you Scott Anderson, Eric Balinski, Jim Berry, Albert V. Bruno, Steve Cates, Susie Chang, Alan Cleland, Tev Dalgic, Sally Dibb, Jude Edwards, José Manuel Ortega Egea, Robert Fast, Russ Haley, Gene Henley, Stavros Kalafatis, Rick Kates, Gary Korenjel, Philip Kotler, Gary Mullet, Marvin Nesbit, Carolyn Saenz, Bruce Seaton, Ben Shapiro, Lyndon Simkin, and Jerry Wind.

Fourth, this book benefited substantially from real-world business experiences gained over the years from hundreds of marketing practitioners. I appreciate what I learned along the way about B2B market segmentation from clients in high-tech, industrial, and service organizations; executive seminar participants at the University of Pittsburgh and Southern Methodist University; academic and trade conferences/presentations; and previous employers such as A.C. Nielsen, Pro-Mark Services, and the Small Business Development Center at Florida International University.

Last, but not least, I especially thank you for reading the *Handbook of Market Segmentation: Strategic Targeting for Business and Technology Firms*!

PART I:
SEGMENTATION PLANNING

Chapter 1

Market Segmentation: An Overview

He who pays the piper can call the tune.

John Ray (1670)

As its name implies, the Tuba Exchange is a North Carolina–based clearinghouse for new and fine used tubas, euphoniums, sousaphones, and accessories. Unlike its major competitors, this firm sells no other musical instruments. Target markets for Tuba Exchange include marching bands, music students, professional musicians, and symphonies. And this niche marketing strategy is effective—sales are growing 20 percent annually.[1]

In fast-changing and increasingly hypercompetitive markets, successful twenty-first-century companies have to be superb segmenters to survive and thrive. Having superior quality goods or services are no longer sufficient. Companies must satisfy discriminating customers who can choose from a multitude of product offerings in a global marketplace. Mass marketing is now a distant memory; today's marketers must aggressively attack target markets and niches that exhibit unique needs and wants. Segmentation-based marketing is the essence of sound business strategy and value creation. For example, the *Farm Journal* responds to advertiser demand and customer desires. The publisher of Farm Journal Media, Steve Custer (personal communication), notes that

> *Farm Journal* has a circulation of more than a half a million. Using a database that identifies all its readers by crops, acreage, livestock raised, geography and even farm practices, it often

publishes well over 1,000 different versions of an issue based on readers' interests.

Segmentation marketing means *knowing your customers,* giving them exactly what they want or may want, building strong relationships with channel affiliates and comarketing partners, and communicating via highly targeted promotional media, e.g., event sponsorships, interactive Web sites, personalized e-mails, trade magazines/shows, etc. Emulating Marriott Hotel's multibrand model, Air Canada recently introduced four subbranded airlines. Air Canada Jazz is the consolidation of several regional airlines: AirBC, Canadian Regional Airlines, Air Ontario, and Air Nova. Air Canada Jetz is a premium charter service for corporate clients and professional sports teams. Tango is a no-frills domestic, long-haul air service (extras are available for a price). Zip flies low fare, short-haul routes in Western Canada.[2]

SEGMENTATION:
THE KEY TO MARKETING SUCCESS

A marketing orientation is based on a customer-driven focus. During the past two decades we have seen the rise of market segmentation in business markets. Introduced into the marketing community by the late Wendell Smith in 1956, a half a century later, segmentation has evolved from an academic concept into a viable "real-world" planning strategy.[3] Everyone has jumped on the market segmentation bandwagon, from global giants to mom-and-pop small businesses. In addition to business and high-tech companies, service organizations, the professions (accounting, legal, etc.), and even nonprofit institutions have embraced the benefits of building marketing muscle.

The Segmentation Imperative

Segmentation is the process of partitioning markets into groups of potential customers with similar needs and/or characteristics who are likely to exhibit similar purchase behavior. It has emerged as a key marketing planning tool and the foundation for effective strategy formulation in American and international companies. The objective of segmentation research is to analyze markets, find niche opportunities, and capitalize on a superior competitive position. This can be accomplished by selecting one or more groups of users as targets for marketing activity and developing unique marketing programs to reach these prime prospects (market segments).

From a practical perspective, *segmentation efforts must be managed* to be successful. It is impossible to pursue every market opportunity so marketers must make strategic choices. First, recognize that everyone is not a prospect for every good or service offered. Remember when IBM dominated the personal computer business? Today, Dell is in command but must carefully watch strategic moves by IBM, Hewlett-Packard, and the Japanese (Sony, Toshiba, etc.), among others.

Second, a firm's product mix has to be controlled for maximum efficiency. Business costs have escalated in all areas (e.g., personnel salaries and benefits, technology and equipment, real estate, plant, materials, and insurance). Ideally, just-in-time production runs should reflect customers' needs and wants for optimal resource utilization. Hence, the marketing challenge is to efficiently match your products to customers' desires and stay one step ahead of your competitors.

SEGMENTATION IN ACTION

Marketing professionals recognize that segmentation is both a science and an art. One can learn a lot about market segmentation analysis through the guidelines and techniques discussed in this book and other valuable published references (as a starting point, see the chapter notes). Also, it is a marketing discipline that can be acquired and enhanced through experience, executive training, observation, and strategic thinking.

There are many alternative methods for segmenting business markets. Many of these approaches are derived from the consumer behavior field. Decision making is impacted by rational and emotional factors (e.g., demographics, geographics, benefits, motivations/needs, purchasing habits, etc.).

Let us assume that a major oil company wants to segment its market. Business marketers can research its customers' customers. A territorial sales analysis of its dealers is a logical starting point. Consumer demographic and socioeconomic measures (age, gender, income, etc.) could be studied. Product consumption (types of unleaded or diesel grade gasoline) can be evaluated. In addition, credit card utilization, brand loyalty/switching patterns, and price sensitivity issues may be insightful for segmenting this market.

As you can see, the options are many; therefore, further research is necessary to determine the best approach(es). The following short examples illustrate six common business segmentation dimensions in action:

1. *Geographic:* A medical instrumentation firm can obtain data from American Hospital Association directories to target hospitals by region and bed size. This approach was valuable for defining markets for a new blood gas analyzer.
2. *Business demographics:* A graphic supplies distributor can easily target advertising agencies by using business demographic variables or firmographics. Using *Advertising Age* and *Adweek* references, the company can find information about the size of prospects (annual billings), media specialization, services offered, major accounts, key personnel, etc.
3. *Adopter categories:* In research I conducted for Cordis Corporation, part of Johnson & Johnson, we identified potential physician adopter segments (progressives, black-box devotees, and show-me's) and nonadopter groups (nonbelievers, no perceived need, and techies) for a proposed medical technology (see Chapter 7). This segmentation technique can be most informative for new product concepts using exploratory studies and qualitative procedures.
4. *Benefits:* What is a firm seeking when buying office copying machines? Is it price, service, special features (enlargement or reduction capabilities, color availability, high volume, speed,

etc.), and/or reputation of the seller (Xerox or Brand X)? A benefit to one customer (enhanced features) may be a drawback to another (higher price).

5. *Product usage:* Business markets can be segmented according to consumption levels of various user groups (heavy, medium, light). In addition, the "best" customers can be identified by several criteria: number of orders, unit sales, revenues, profitability, share of customer volume, etc.

6. *Purchasing approaches:* Dell's strategy of seeking sophisticated buyers and large accounts not requiring much "hand-holding" (i.e., limited technical support) is sound target marketing.

SEGMENTATION OPTIONS

A company has two basic strategic choices: (1) to segment the market or (2) to treat the entire market as potential customers for its goods or services. This latter option means that the firm uses an undifferentiated marketing strategy. There are few (if any) companies that can benefit from this approach. One can argue that utilities can employ this strategy, since you must have their service in an essentially monopolistic environment. But even that is not true anymore. In today's free market, you do not have to use the electricity provided by your local power company if you do not choose to (options include solar panels, windmills, and other environmentally friendly energy sources). In the once uncontested telecommunications industry, AT&T now faces formidable competition in all sectors in which it competes (long distance, local, wireless).

Despite the fact that undifferentiation is for virtually no one, too many companies still treat their marketing as if everyone is a likely customer, rather than targeting those who are the *most likely* prospects for their products. Recognizing the great diversity in the marketplace, it is clearly desirable to segment markets to improve marketing performance. By segmentation we mean the development of unique marketing strategies for the various needs of the marketplace. Segmentation options include differentiation, concentration, and atomization (segment-of-one marketing). Business Segmentation Insight 1 reviews the usage and effectiveness of business-to-business (B2B) market selection strategies in the United States and United Kingdom.

BUSINESS SEGMENTATION INSIGHT 1: SEGMENTATION RESEARCH FINDINGS IN HIGH-TECH AND INDUSTRIAL MARKETS

Example 1

A national segmentation study was conducted in technology-based industries by this writer.[4] Two hundred three top-level U.S. marketing executives in nine industries (automation, biotechnology, computer hardware, computer software, electronics, medical equipment and instrumentation, pharmaceuticals, photonics, and telecommunications) participated in this research project. A breakdown by annual sales revenue indicated that 110 firms were small (less than $10 million sales) and ninety-three were medium/large (greater than $10 million sales). Three key market selection findings from the study are summarized here:

1. High-technology firms were dependent on a primary market segment that accounted for 69 percent of their business.
2. Nearly two-thirds of the firms (130, 65 percent) used a differentiation strategy; the balance was split fairly evenly between an undifferentiated approach (36, 18 percent) and a concentrated strategy (35, 17 percent).
3. Segmenters (concentrated and differentiated marketers) were found to be significantly more effective target marketers than nonsegmenters (undifferentiated marketers).

Example 2

A pharmaceutical sector segmentation study was conducted ($n = 107$) in the United Kingdom by Kalafatis and Cheston.[5] They found that 72 percent of the firms segmented the market (28 percent of the firms did not; they used the undifferentiated approach). Macro variables such as end use or application (61 percent cited this variable) were most frequently used for single-stage segmentation, practiced by 15 percent of the firms. Usage variables such as purchase volume and purchasing situations were incorporated into the two-stage approach by 26 percent of the companies. Sophisticated segmenters employed three-stage segmentation where price sensitivity became an important variable (this more complex approach was employed by 31 percent of the sample).

Example 3

A four-industry study of large companies in the United Kingdom by Kalafatis and Tsogas[6] found that the quality of service required was the most effective segmentation base in the computer software and plastics markets; this variable ranked second in chemicals and cement/concrete (benefits derived was ranked first). Other important variables found in the top-five lists for two or more industrial sectors included end use application, level of risk, technical requirements, and speed of delivery.

Differentiation

If a firm identifies and actively markets its products or services to two or more segments of the market based on varied customer needs, a differentiation strategy is being used. The computer distributor that separately targets business professionals, retailers, and small businesses is employing a differentiation approach to marketing PCs, peripherals, software, and supplies. A distinction needs to be made between market and product differentiation. Market differentiation (a segmentation strategy) is customer oriented and is dependent upon market demand, while product differentiation (not a segmentation strategy) is supply side oriented.

Concentration

A concentration strategy means that the firm decides to serve one of several potential segments of the market. Under a concentration segmentation approach, a computer dealer may direct its products and services to small businesses only, ignoring potential opportunities in the business professional or retailer segments. Concentrated marketing is less expensive than differentiated marketing and is the appropriate choice for a new business with limited resources or a firm diversifying in a market outside of its core business.

Atomization (Segment-of-One Marketing)

This segmentation option has received tremendous attention by business strategists during the past decade. Atomization has many names and variants: customerization, interactive segmentation, mass customization, micromarketing, one-to-one marketing, and personalization. Database marketing, flexible manufacturing systems, integrated distribution systems, and relationship marketing are also important tools used by segment-of-one or finer-segmentation marketers.[7]

Regardless of the chosen nomenclature, this approach breaks down the market to the finest level of detail—individual customers. Table 1.1 compares traditional segmentation (differentiation) and atomization.

An atomization strategy can be used as a stand-alone technique or in conjunction with differentiation or concentration. It is particularly

TABLE 1.1. Differences Between Segmentation and Atomization

Strategic Focus	Segmentation	Segment-of-One Marketing
Market segments	Groups	Individuals
Marketing mix	Same for entire segment	Tailored to each customer
Promotional strategy	Mass communication	Individual addressability
Promotional emphasis	Awareness creation, preference	Tailoring offerings to customer needs/interests, retention
Marketing flexibility	Largely inflexible within a given time period	Highly flexible and adaptive
Sales initiatives	Phone orders, sales calls, Web orders	Real time ordering more likely

Source: Adapted from David M. Gardner, "Segmentation Strategy in the Interactive Marketing Era," in K. Grant and I. Walker (eds.), *Proceedings of the Seventh Annual Bi-Annual World Marketing Congress*, Melbourne, Australia, July 1-6, 1995, pp. 8-31–8-37.

appropriate for manufacturers of specialized and costly equipment (e.g., multimillion dollar supercomputers), creating marketing programs for government markets (such as the defense industry), exploiting large-scale marketing databases, and staving off competition by offering extended product features or product lines.

As an example, Lutron Electronics developed a mass-customization strategy to successfully withstand a competitive threat by General Electric. Lutron's deep product mix (11,000 items), modularized approach, and in-depth knowledge of its interior designer and architect customers allowed it to customize lighting systems to individual specifications while maintaining low costs.[8]

While customized segmentation is precision target marketing and offers much promise to twenty-first-century companies, management must be aware of its shortcomings: increased costs, technological challenges, overchoice for decision makers, and implementation and measurement difficulties. While total atomization can work extremely well for some highly sophisticated companies, Russell Haley (a leading segmentation scholar and the founder of the benefit segmentation approach) astutely points out that "mass customization can easily lead to mass confusion."[9] Professors Elliott of Australia and Glynn of Ireland echoed Haley's view. They contend that "the proposition that all firms will be able to customize their offer for each individual customer is patently unrealistic, as, for example the prospect of negotiating your individual train journey with the engine driver!"[10]

The reality is that in most market situations, traditional segmentation still works and works quite well; invariably, customers have a limited number of similar needs and wants that can be sated by providing sets of similar products/services that create superior value. Segment-of-one marketing can be a powerful strategic differentiator and should be used, as applicable, too. A review of the differences in the various market selection strategies (including niche marketing, which is discussed in the next section) is summarized in Table 1.2.

TABLE 1.2. Market Selection Options

Number of Segments Targeted	Segmentation Strategies	Comments
Zero	Undifferentiation	Mass-marketing approach, no targeting
One	Concentration or single niche	Highly focused marketing
Two or more	Differentiation, multiple niches	A sound approach for competing in several market arenas
Dozens to thousands	Atomization	Requires one-to-one marketing strategy; dependent on a strong marketing information system

NICHEMANSHIP: SEGMENTED MARKETING AT ITS BEST

In 343 B.C., Demosthenes, a noted Athenian statesman and orator, said, "small opportunities are often the beginning of great enterprises." Market niches are small segments that offer incremental business today and, perhaps, vast potential tomorrow. They allow highly specialized marketers to be big fish in small ponds. Niche marketing is a form of concentrated target marketing. Strategies that companies use to find their niche include geographic focus, demographic profiling, customer preferences, product/service modification, alternative distribution channels, customer service variations, technological developments, targeted communications, and variable pricing.

While we often think of small firms as nichers or guerilla marketers, Tevfik Dalgic explains that large companies can effectively use niche marketing principles and practices, too. He adds that IBM, Johnson & Johnson, and Philips are by no means gorillas (slow-moving giants); these global leaders all utilize niche marketing strategies in their respective worldwide business units.[11]

In a segmentation research initiative that I facilitated for Intel, marketing managers explored more than forty potential niches. The goal was to find a few new product applications to augment their primary market segments and strategic marketing plan (discussed further in Chapter 9).

Nichemanship is the process whereby a company integrates marketing and management activities to optimize its competitive market position. A segmentation-derived positioning strategy for a focal customer target is a major part of nichemanship. Here are four other characteristics of a market nicher:

1. The company determines those products/services that it can best offer given its distinct competencies, competition, and customer needs (truly market-oriented).
2. It designs specialized goods and services to meet identified market demands.
3. By focusing its energies on specific target markets, it is more efficient than its larger counterparts in satisfying its customer base.
4. Change is sought—such firms are not looking to be like everyone else but, rather, seek new and better ways to conduct business.

Realize that niche marketers are trendsetters/spotters, market innovators, and creative marketing strategists.

True niche-based firms also recognize the value of sound research and stand the test of time. Philip Kotler details the characteristics of attractive market niches: customers in the niche have a distinct set of needs; they will pay a premium to the firm that best satisfies their niches; the niche is not likely to attract competitors; the nicher gains economies of scale through specialization; and the niche has growth, profit, and size potential.[12]

Apple Computer and Alltel are two firms that have excelled as niche marketers. Apple was a pioneer in the personal computing industry. Once an industry leader, Apple has transformed itself to survive as a niche player with global market share of less than 5 percent. Their user-friendly Macintosh and iMac products have been used by millions worldwide as an alternative to the Wintel PC standard. Although they have recently demonstrated a strong commitment toward marketing digital consumer electronics such as the iPod, iPhoto, and iMovie, desktop publishing (design, graphics, media, etc.) and education have remained as Apple's core markets over the years.[13]

Alltel, an Arkansas-based telecommunications company has avoided head-to-head competition with the six leading wireless service providers by focusing on rural subscribers. This niche marketing strategy has netted them about 7 million customers.[14] Box 1.1 provides ten key questions to assess how well your firm practices niche marketing.

BOX 1.1. Are You a Good Niche Marketer?

1. Do you know your firm's strengths, weaknesses, and competitive advantage?
2. Do you understand your customer, inside and out?
3. Is your company dependent on one or a limited number of customers? Do most of your sales come from a single product?
4. Have you developed an ongoing customer information system? Does it measure sales, profits, and market response links?
5. How well do you know your competition? (e.g., Why do customers use competitive products? How can you get them to switch?)
6. What is your positioning strategy? Have you developed and communicated a clear image for your product/product line? How is your product differentiated from your rivals'?
7. Have you created your own safe haven in the market? (Try not to compete with yourself, but create high-entry barriers for others.)
8. Are your resources spread too thin? (Watch for overexpansion, attacking too many niches.)
9. Is your marketing program synergistic? Is it consistent with your financial, management, operations, and R&D strategies?
10. Are you monitoring shifts in the marketplace and responding quickly to them?

Source: Adapted from Tevfik Dalgic and Maartin Leeuw, "Niche Marketing Revisited: Theoretical and Practical Issues," in Michael Levy and Dhruv Grewal (eds.), *Academy of Marketing Science Proceedings,* Miami Beach, May 26-29, 1993, pp. 137-145.

THE BENEFITS OF SEGMENTATION

The overall objective of using a market segmentation strategy is to improve your company's competitive position and better serve the needs of your customers. Some specific objectives may include increased sales (in units and dollars), improved market share, and enhanced image/reputation. This is not to say that it is impossible to accomplish these goals using mass marketing tactics. However, by focusing in on areas that your firm can best serve, it is more likely to prosper. An undifferentiated strategy is the shotgun approach to marketing, while segmentation is the high-powered rifle. The following are four major benefits of market segmentation analysis and strategy:

1. *Designing responsive products to meet the needs of the marketplace:* Through researching customer preferences—an essential component of segmentation analysis—the company moves toward accomplishing the marketing concept (customer satisfaction at a profit). The firm places the customer first and designs and refines its product/service mix to satisfy the needs of the market.
2. *Determining effective and cost-efficient promotional strategies:* As a planning tool, segmentation identification and analysis is extremely valuable in building a customer database and designing the firm's communication mix. Appropriate advertising campaigns can be developed that are targeted to the right media vehicles. This marketing investment can be supplemented by focused public relations initiatives and sales promotion methods. In addition to mass promotional thrusts, the personal sales process can be greatly improved by providing sales representatives with background customer research, recommended sales appeals, and ongoing support.
3. *Evaluating market competition, in particular the company's market position:* Today's markets are characterized by intense domestic and global competition. A segmentation study explores the firm's market position, i.e., how the company is perceived by its customers and potential customers relative to the

competition. Segmentation research provides a competitive intelligence mechanism to assess how well your company compares to industry standards. In addition, this analysis is useful for detecting trends in changing and volatile markets.

4. *Providing insight on present marketing strategies:* It is important to periodically reevaluate your present marketing strategies to try to capitalize on new opportunities and circumvent potential threats. Market segmentation research is also useful in exploring new markets (e.g., secondary, smaller, or fringe markets). Furthermore, segmentation findings provide a *systematic approach for controlled market coverage,* as opposed to the hit-or-miss, random efforts of mass or unfocused marketing.

In sum, segmentation analysis provides that necessary research base upon which all other marketing strategies can be successfully formulated and executed. Is your company using market segmentation techniques effectively? Segmentation Skillbuilder 1 identifies fifteen key issues to explore further to help you answer this critical strategic marketing question.

LIMITATIONS OF SEGMENTATION

The picture is not totally rosy, however, and the marketer must be cognizant of some potential shortcomings of segmentation analysis, such as the following.

Increased Costs

A segmentation-based strategy is more costly than a mass-marketing approach. For example, differentiation often implies new product/ service offerings, several promotional campaigns, channel development and expansion, increased Internet expenses, and additional resources for implementation and control. On the plus side, target marketing means limited waste (advertising reaches prospects not suspects) and improved marketing performance.

SEGMENTATION SKILLBUILDER 1:
HOW WELL IS YOUR COMPANY
USING SEGMENTATION TECHNIQUES?

1. Does your company segment the market? If not, why not?
2. What strategy is used—differentiation, concentration, or atomization?
3. Has your company established a niche marketing program?
4. What segments/niches are you trying to serve? How successful are you at meeting this objective?
5. What is your typical customer profile?
6. Are target market definitions based on research?
7. What dimensions (methods) are used to segment markets?
8. When was your last segmentation analysis conducted?
9. How frequently are updates obtained?
10. What is your budget for segmentation analysis?
11. Are product decisions based on segmentation research?
12. Are promotional decisions based on segmentation research?
13. Are pricing and distribution decisions based on segmentation?
14. Is segmentation analysis used in assessing competition, trends, and changes in the marketplace?
15. Is segmentation analysis used to evaluate your present marketing efforts (e.g., markets to pursue)?

Requires a Major Corporate Commitment

A marketing orientation requires a strong commitment by the firm. This includes support in the areas of personnel, resources to hire marketing consultants, time investment of management, and the willingness to act on prescribed recommendations. This transition may take months. The effectiveness or ineffectiveness of segmentation studies is limited by management's ability to implement strategic implications (watch for blaming junior-level marketing associates, the consultants, or the advertising agency).

Realize that segmentation research is not a remedy for other marketing deficiencies. The best segmentation information in the world is worthless unless it is supported by consistent product, promotional, pricing, distribution, and customer service strategies; these must be regularly evaluated and revised, as situations dictate. In addition, market segmentation strategies are not a panacea for other organizational limitations (e.g., financial, operational, managerial, research and development, etc.).

Provides Composite Not Individual Profiles

Although segmentation research provides meaningful marketing information, it explains expected segmentwide (not individual) purchase behavior. While customers may appear to be similar based on demographic, need, and/or usage profiles, marketers must still appeal to specific buyers through direct-marketing tactics and personal-selling initiatives.

As an example, two industrial purchasing agents may both be male, forty-five years old, have an MBA, and earn $85,000 annually. By using basic demographic analysis only, the marketer may erroneously stereotype these buyers as similar prospects. In reality, they may have different interests, attitudes, and perspectives on life, as well as varying corporate circumstances with which they must contend (e.g., business cultures, decision-making influences, purchasing policies and constraints, risk uncertainty, etc.). Behavioral research via adopter categories, benefit segments, organizational psychographics, or usage analysis can assist management by presenting more complete pictures of market situations.

SEGMENTATION:
SOME MISUNDERSTANDINGS RESOLVED

There are three major misconceptions about market segmentation held by many business professionals. These are explored and clarified in this brief section.

- *Myth 1: Market segmentation is a partitioning process.* The overall effect of segmentation is to divide markets into two or more manageable submarkets. However, in reality, segmentation is a gathering process, since potential customers are assembled together by commonalities in specific characteristics to form segments.

- *Myth 2: Segmentation is only a process or technique.* This is another half-truth. Although segmentation is research based, its real impact comes from its role as a strategic marketing variable. Market segmentation is the primary strategic element in a company's marketing plan. It is the foundation upon which all other marketing actions can be based.
- *Myth 3: Everyone is part of a market segment.* Although this might be an ideal situation for the marketer, in actuality, all customers do not fit neatly into a market segment. It is likely that a small percentage of the population will be unclassifiable based on the specified segment formation criteria. This aberrant "other" group has one or more inconsistencies in key segmentation decision characteristics; hence, they are not good prospects for concentrated marketing activity.

One cautionary note: the "other" group should be limited in size (less than 10 percent of the market). In one study, I observed an "other" category of 40 percent; this segment was larger than the three identified segments! Such categorization was inadequate and indicated that further subsegmentation was necessary.

SUMMARY

To compete successfully in the fast-changing and challenging global markets of the twenty-first century, business and technology firms (large and small) should use segmentation techniques and strategies to find their competitive advantage. Relevant market selection options are differentiation, concentration, and atomization.

Market differentiation means that the firm designs two or more marketing strategies to serve designated segments based on differing customer characteristics and needs. Concentrated marketers recognize the diversity of the marketplace but choose to attack a single target market opportunity—this is generally cost efficient and enables management to focus on what they do best. An atomization approach develops individualized marketing programs for each key prospect or customer—although costly, this strategy may prove very successful. Also, do not forget the value of niche marketing in your segmentation planning.

Segmentation-driven marketing strategy helps companies design responsive products, develop effective promotional tactics and campaigns, gauge competitive positions, and fine-tune current marketing initiatives. In spite of numerous benefits, marketers must also recognize that segmentation strategy is generally more costly than mass marketing and necessitates a major commitment by management to customer-oriented planning, research, implementation, and control.

Chapter 2

Market Definition and Segmentation in B2B Markets

I asked each of the businesses to redefine its markets and give us a page or two of "fresh thinking" . . . GE went from a "market definition" of about $115 billion in 1981 to over $1 trillion today, providing plenty of room for growth.

Jack Welch (2001)

General Electric's power systems business viewed its services as primarily supplying spares and doing repairs on GE technology—defined in this manner, it held 63 percent of a $2.7 billion market. A redefinition of the market to include total power plant maintenance meant that this unit had only a 10 percent share of a $17 billion market. Broadening the market even further to include fuel, power, inventory, asset management, and financial services resulted in a potential $170 billion market with GE holding about a 1 percent share of the market. According to Welch, this boundaryless thinking helped the company grow from $70 billion in revenues in 1995 to $130 billion in 2000.[1]

THE MARKET DEFINITION CHALLENGE

As the previous GE example illustrates, to win customers, companies must clearly understand the presegmented markets in which they

This chapter builds on a model/ideas first presented in Art Weinstein, *Defining Your Market: Winning Strategies for High-Tech, Industrial, and Service Firms* (Binghamton, NY: The Haworth Press, 1998), pp. 99-107.

compete. This must occur prior to designing target market strategies. Vandermerwe explains that managers should pursue customer-activity arenas based on the results that buyers seek. She adds that "market spaces are not products like cars but activity arenas like personal mobility; not personal computers but global-networking capabilities; not fuel oil but integrated energy assurance."[2]

How important are market definition decisions? Smart executives must consider the strategic and tactical consequences to their firm. The impact of effective or ineffective market definitions is evidenced by the recent actions (or inaction) of nine leading companies (see Table 2.1).

Hamel and Prahalad explain that it is now increasingly difficult to define precisely where an industry begins and ends. Realize that markets develop from existing, emerging, and even imagined business opportunities. They add that many unexploited market opportunities are found based on unserved customer types and unarticulated customer needs. Products such as automobile navigation systems, cell phones, fax machines, and satellite receivers were developed in the factory first rather than specifically requested by the marketplace.[3]

Often, working market definitions are too simplistic. This approach tends to be limiting and stifles creativity. For example, some companies define their markets solely by geographic area (the Pacific Northwest), product (pumps and motors), industry (telecommunications), state of action (frequent flyers), or state of mind (techies).

Richer, more comprehensive market definitions are desirable; an integrated, multidimensional view of the market is advocated. For example, a European manufacturer of agricultural and construction equipment analyzed *products* such as backhoe loaders, bulldozers, cranes, dump trucks, excavators, fork lifts, spreaders, tractors, wheeled loading shovels, etc.; *customer sectors* such as agriculture, civil engineering, contractors, earthmoving, extraction, house building, landscaping, public utilities, tool hire, waste disposal, etc.; and *countries* as part of a segment evaluation matrix.[4] Business Segmentation Insight 2 shows how business mission and vision statements can assist management in defining markets.

TABLE 2.1. Market Definition and Corporate Performance

Company	Action/Inaction	Business Impact
Cisco	Emphasizing network solutions in data, video, and voice applications	Collaborated with resellers to provide value-added solutions, leading to higher prices and enhanced margins
DuPont	Evolving from a major chemical producer into a value-added seller of information products and services	Seeking new business ventures emphasizing services and information
Hewlett-Packard	Increased focus on core business (hardware/technology) products	Divested Agilent Technologies; acquired Compaq
IBM	"Global solutions for a small planet" promotional campaign helped power a change from a technology company to a business/industry problem solver	E-business bolstered IBM's fast-growing services and consulting divisions
Motorola University	Shift in corporate training to customized knowledge "chunks" rather than traditional courses and modules	Able to provide Motorola's employees, suppliers, and customers information access and applications— "right knowledge, right now"
Novell	Acquired Cambridge Technology	Moved from being a seller of network operating systems to software infrastructure/tools, Web products, and consulting solutions
St. Joe Company	Sold paper mill, box factories, and sugar holdings	Became a real estate development giant in Northwest Florida, the largest private landowner in the state
Xerox	Unsure if a copier, document, information, or printing company	Substantial declines in key financial indicators, massive layoffs, and divestitures of SBUs
Yahoo	Online portal company became unclear of its business premise; found itself too dependent on selling ads to fading Internet firms	Dot-com crash cut revenue stream by 75 percent; company now refocused on selling new business and consumer services

BUSINESS SEGMENTATION INSIGHT 2:
MISSION, VISION, AND MARKET DEFINITION

Market-focused companies integrate market definitions into corporate and business unit planning frameworks to guide programs, processes, products, and people. Market definition provides a springboard for the development of mission and vision statements that work rather than just look good on paper. Business performance demonstrates that mission statements are effective. A study of *Business Week*'s Global 1000 companies showed that those with mission statements reported an average return on stockholder equity of 16.1 percent versus 9.7 percent for those which lacked this strategic planning document.[5]

A worldwide study of top executives' perceptions of twenty-five hot management tools by Bain & Company showed that mission and vision statements were the second most widely used tool (70 percent utilization rate) but only yielded the seventh highest satisfaction score. In contrast, customer segmentation was used by only 50 percent of the companies surveyed (it was ninth based on tool usage) but it had the third highest satisfaction rate.[6] Three implications of this research are that (1) businesses can do a better job in articulating mission and vision statements, (2) more companies need to use segmentation analysis, and (3) these two tools should work together to create a customer-centric organization.

Effective mission statements must be clear, relevant, inspiring, enduring, and adaptable. Furthermore, missions should be brief but complete, provide strategic direction, present the big picture, lead to results, and answer such basic questions as these:

- What business are we really in?
- How is our business changing?
- What other businesses do we need to be in?
- Who are our customers?
- What do our customers want?
- How do we create, maximize, and deliver value to our customers?
- What is our business philosophy?
- How are we different (and better) from our competitors?

While the mission states what your business is today, the vision statement is future directed and should revitalize the organization; it looks at your business tomorrow—five- to ten-year views typically work well, although many Japanese companies use a much longer planning horizon. A vision may represent an ideal scenario, but it is doable if the organization's people perform to their capabilities. BellSouth's vision is to be the customer's best connection to communications, information, and entertainment.

While vision statements can be a highly valuable market planning tool, research shows that there are relatively few truly visionary leaders. One study reported that only 5 percent of companies had strong vision statements and less than 1 percent had ones that were effectively communicated to their people.[7] Vision statements sometimes fail because they are viewed as fads. Strong companies do not fall into the "searching for the magical answer" trap.

Ideally, companies should aspire toward *market and customer ownership*. Since effective market definitions are unique, antitrust concerns are not necessarily a threat. Market ownership implies the identification of *distinctive business opportunities* (DBOs). The implication is that it is better to control a majority of a well-defined market sector (be the big fish in a small pond) than to have a small share of a broad market (be the small fish in a giant lake). In the former case, customers will place your organization at the head of their mental list as to which company can best satisfy their needs. This high degree of top-of-mind awareness is unlikely to exist in the latter case.

According to Sherdan, firms should be able to assess six key factors—customer segment, product/service, needs and values, channel, functions, and geography—in defining distinct businesses.[8] The capability of owning customers is the key to achieving a sustainable competitive advantage. Companies such as Dell, FedEx, Merck, Microsoft, Southwest Airlines, and others have embraced this strategy.

Source: Adapted and updated from Art Weinstein, *Defining Your Market: Winning Strategies for High-Tech, Industrial, and Service Firms* (Binghamton, NY: The Haworth Press, 1998), pp. 24-27.

A STRATEGIC MARKET DEFINITION FRAMEWORK

Markets can be defined in many ways. For example, Kotler comments that marketers are concerned with available, penetrated, potential, qualified, served, and total markets.[9] While this concept of submarkets is quite helpful from a planning and management perspective, the terminology is, at times, confusing. Other research found that markets consist of a blending of customer needs, customer groups, competition, products, and technologies.[10] Building on these ideas, a pragmatic market definition model consisting of three levels and nine components is developed and explained in this chapter (see Figure 2.1).

Level 1: The Relevant Market

As Figure 2.1 shows, the initial "big" objective is to adequately define your relevant market (4); this is the market appropriate for an organization given its resources, objectives, and environment. Identifying the geographic market (1), the trade area an organization serves, is a relatively easy first step. This is accomplished by using market scope (e.g., local, regional, national, international, or global) and other geographic market measures (e.g., census classifications, standardized market areas [such as Arbitron's Areas of Dominant Influence, or ADIs], and customer density). This is discussed further in Chapter 4.

Product market identification (2) is also relatively straightforward. Organizations can readily list the goods, services, and ideas they have available for sale. As an example, my consulting practice consists of the following services:

- *Training:* seminars, speeches, and customized educational programs on segmentation/niche marketing and market definition
- *Research:* segmentation studies, surveys, focus groups, and market profiles
- *Strategic consulting:* marketing audits, marketing plans, market redefinition, target market strategy development, and visioning sessions

Level 1: The Relevant Market

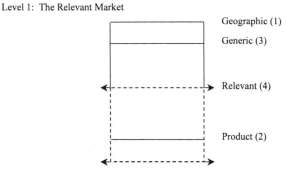

Geographic (1)

Generic (3)

Relevant (4)

Product (2)

Level 2: The "Defined" Market

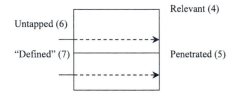

Relevant (4)

Untapped (6)

"Defined" (7)

Penetrated (5)

Level 3: The Target Market(s)

Segmented (8)

Target (9)

FIGURE 2.1. Strategic Market Definition Framework

Explicating the generic market (3) is a useful exercise to ensure that management is considering various and diverse marketing opportunities. While marketing myopia (narrow, product-oriented thinking) is avoided, a large market definition (typical of the generic market) may lead to mass marketing mentality and make a company's efforts and resources seem almost insignificant.

Defining the relevant market (4) provides a reality check for the organization; here a market definition is specified that is larger than the product market, but smaller than the generic market. The relevant market yields realistic boundaries to guide the management and marketing operations of your business. As an example, research found that the choice of a relevant market in the hospital services industry affects the technology adoption of electronic fetal monitors and centralized energy management systems.[11]

    Sell-Soft competes in the sales automation (SA) industry. SA systems utilize computers to manage processes in the sales cycle from lead generation to postsale service functions. Sales automation products can be used for contact management, sales forecasting, service reports, integrated marketing management, and other applications. Sell-Soft's management can use Figure 2.2 to guide future business expansion strategies. Once the relevant market is established, we proceed to the next level in the market definition framework—the defined market.

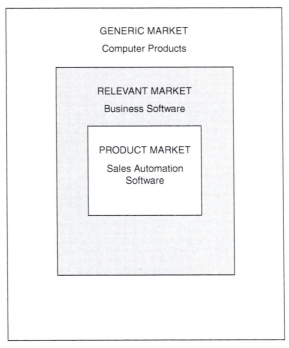

FIGURE 2.2. Sell-Soft's Relevant Market (*Note:* Company name has been disguised.)

Level 2: The Defined Market

Using the relevant market (4) as a departure point, we are now in position to fine-tune our market definition. The firm should assess its current customer base, or penetrated market (5), and noncustomers, or untapped market (6). Often the defined market (7) will include most of your current customers (although some customers are not profitable to serve and you can afford to lose them) as well as many new prospects.

Nypro, a plastics-injection company, took the market redefinition mandate quite seriously. As part of its corporate strategy to develop partnerships with a select number of large companies, Nypro phased out small customers. This plan reduced its customer base from 800 to 80! Half of the remaining accounts generated over a $1 million in annual sales, with the other forty approaching that figure.[12]

Although Nypro's customer intimacy strategy made sense for them, do not think that you should say goodbye to 90 percent of your customers or just try to hit homeruns (gain/retain million-dollar accounts). Rather, the willingness to occasionally walk away from "bad" customers is not a heretical view; it may be a sound strategy to allow your company to do a better job servicing solid, existing accounts and new, promising customers. For example, an electrical components manufacturer used strategic market analysis to win large-lot, price-sensitive buyers while selectively pricing itself out of a small-lot, specialty business that required overservicing. A revised, Level 2 market definition factors in annual growth rates, minimal acceptable sales thresholds, anticipated servicing levels, or other modifiers.

Level 3: The Target Markets

At Level 3, we take the "presegmented" market definition (7) and apply segmentation bases (e.g., geodemographics, benefits, usage, etc.) to identify groups of customers with similar characteristics or needs that are likely to exhibit similar purchase behavior; this is our segmented market (8). The specific target markets (9) selected to pursue with differentiated marketing strategies are the final element of the market definition model.

As an example, Winnebago learned that selling travel trailers (a new business venture that failed) was very different from selling motor homes (its core business). The customer groups are dissimilar, trailers are more price competitive, and they do not require service, whereas motor homes do.[13]

MARKET DEFINITION APPLICATIONS BASED ON THE FRAMEWORK

Most small firms take a product-oriented rather than customer-centered view of the market. Consider a company that says it is in the emergency vehicle lighting business (product market).[14] This business competes in a tiny part of the aggregate lighting market (generic market) and in a small sector of the emergency lighting systems market (relevant market).

One prospective new product that management can consider is emergency lighting for mass transit. Since this initiative is located in the relevant market zone, it is likely that the firm will miss this potentially lucrative opportunity. This market myopia is caused by zeroing in on its current product market and ignoring new, but related business profit centers.

From a segmentation perspective, the emergency vehicle lighting market (product market) consists of ambulance, fire, police, tow truck, and utilities industries. Market size and competition will dictate which target markets/niches to pursue. As one ingredient in this business decision, the emergency vehicle lighting firm must realize that there are only about 500 fire trucks produced a year, while there are approximately 100 times that number of police cars manufactured annually.

As the previous example illustrates, not all of the nine market components play a critical role in every analysis. An integrated and systematic market definition process, as proposed, can help companies more effectively understand their customers, competitors, and changes in their environment. This knowledge means increased marketing performance. Table 2.2 provides a comparison of how two companies defined their markets based on the three-level market definition model. Segmentation Skillbuilder 2 gives you an opportunity to strategize about your organization's relevant, defined, and target markets.

SEGMENTATION SKILLBUILDER 2:
DEFINING YOUR MARKET—A THREE-LEVEL APPROACH

Using the three-level, nine-part market definition framework (see Figure 2.1), how might you define your market?

Market Terminology   **Proposed Market Definition**
  1. Geographic   _____
  2. Product market   _____
  3. Generic market   _____
  4. Relevant market   _____
  5. Penetrated market   _____
  6. Untapped market   _____
  7. Defined market   _____
  8. Segmented market   _____
  9. Target market(s)   _____

Management Challenge

Schedule a day-long visioning session with the executive team to share with them your initial market view, solicit input on refining the various market definitions, disseminate this information to other managers and key employees, and develop strategies to best serve your target markets.

SUMMARY

A market consists of customers (actual and potential), needs, products, technologies, and competitors. One of the most difficult challenges managers face is how to define relevant and presegmented

TABLE 2.2. Two Examples of Market Definition

Market Definition	Steel Company	CPA Firm
Geographic market	North America	Midwestern United States
Product market	Fabrication	Audit, tax services
Generic market	Sheared/bent plate	Financial services
Relevant market	Extra-long and fifty-foot sections	Business consulting
Penetrated market	Northeastern U.S. customers of construction equipment	Existing accounting clients
Untapped market	NAFTA steel users	Nonusers (clients and nonclients) of business consulting
Defined market	NAFTA construction equipment manufacturers	Growth-oriented, closely held businesses; new IPO companies
Segmented market	Cranes, concrete pumps, off-road construction, road construction	Businesses following a growth strategy
Target market(s)	Cranes	Sales growth > 10 percent yearly; acquisition-minded companies

markets. A market definition too narrow limits potential opportunities; one too large leads to mass-marketing thinking and can make an organization's efforts and resources seem almost insignificant. This chapter reviewed useful market terminology and explained how a field-tested, multipart framework can be used for developing practical and optimal market definitions and segmentation approaches for business and high-tech companies. Ten segmentation planning and research guidelines are developed in the next chapter.

Chapter 3

Segmentation Planning and Research Guidelines for Business Marketers

It was not the possibility of planning as such which has been questioned . . . but the possibility of successful planning.

F. A. Hayek (1935)

According to William D. Neal, the founder of Atlanta-based SDR Consulting, the use of segmentation research by companies has made positive strides in the past decade. He adds, "Business managers have relearned the benefits of target marketing. Most marketers now recognize that simplistic segmentation schemes based on demographics, geography or SIC codes are suboptimal at best—and disastrous at worse."[1]

Today's leaders dominate submarkets that have specialized needs and wants. While top executives often advocate being market oriented and customer focused, I have found that the majority of B2B companies, high-technology firms, and service organizations (large and small) fail to utilize target marketing to its fullest potential. In spite of the many advances in segmentation theory and practice over its nearly fifty-year evolution, many firms still base their marketing plans on cursory, incomplete, or intuitive market analyses. However, used effectively, *strategic segmentation*—based on sound planning and research—provides a strong foundation for increasing sales and improving overall marketing performance.

Realize that business markets are continually impacted by changing technologies, demanding customers, regulatory reform, global competition, escalating costs, time pressures, and a myriad of other environmental factors. In the daily course of "fighting fires," it is easy to see how excellent people and great companies can quickly become sidetracked from their corporate purpose.

SEGMENTATION ROADBLOCKS

Getting "close to the customer" has become a rallying cry for successful companies. Market segmentation is a key ingredient in the transformation of business cultures. Organizations now use segmentation strategies to find/attract new customers and enhance existing customer relationships. Unfortunately, in many cases, segmentation studies are not practical enough to have a major impact on overall strategic direction and marketing performance.

Why does market segmentation often fail to achieve its much heralded expectations in the business world? Here are three primary reasons:

1. Relatively few individuals have the understanding, expertise, and authority to incorporate this technique into a company's marketing plan; hence, underanalysis of a market is common. Occasionally, companies may overanalyze their markets. One leading statewide, health care insurance provider commissioned eighteen different segmentation studies over a five-year period; yet, none of these were turned into strategy!

2. Many segmentation analyses emphasize methodological and statistical procedures over substance. The end product of such a study is a complex model understood only by the researcher and not implemented by management—the classic "report on the executive's shelf" syndrome. (In contrast, a document with smudge marks, coffee stains, and/or dog-eared edges is a working plan.) Appropriate analytical techniques for segmentation analysis are reviewed later in this chapter.

3. Marketing research can be expensive; management may not perceive the benefits of market segmentation analysis relative to its cost. In one project I did for a major medical device manufacturer, senior executives authorized the first phase of a segmenta-

tion study (an industry/competitive market profile) once they realized that the investment for the study was only the equivalent of the cost of two cardiac pacemakers (about $5,000).

The Remedy: Design a Practical Segmentation Study

To enhance the value of market segmentation and provide "hands-on" decision-oriented information that is readily translatable into marketing strategy, practicality is of the essence. Management needs to be actively involved in the study. Coordination, cooperation, and a close working relationship among the entire marketing team (e.g., top management, product managers, researchers, strategists, etc.) are vital to the success of a practical segmentation study. In my consulting activities I seek input from all levels of marketing management, not just the professionals I am working with directly. Management then "buys in" and recognizes that the project is a worthwhile marketing activity rather than just an expense.

How do you introduce or improve segmentation procedures and activities in your firm?[2] Effective, cost-efficient, and profitable segmentation analysis requires the following five inputs:

1. *Superior planning:* Objectives may focus on segment identification, segment description, segment validation, etc. Systematic planning is stressed. A ten-point managerial framework emphasizing planning and research guidelines leads to effective segmentation studies. This is reviewed in the next section.
2. *Solid research:* Choose the optimal blend of primary, secondary, syndicated, database, and Internet research sources.
3. *Selecting the "right" segmentation dimensions:* Options include adopter categories, benefits, firmographics, geographics, purchasing approaches, usage, etc.
4. *Strategy development:* Objectives include target market selection, positioning, nichemanship, and formulating the proper marketing mix based on product, pricing, promotion, distribution, and e-marketing tools.
5. *Implementation and control:* Implement, evaluate, and revise the segmentation plan.

USING PLANNING AND RESEARCH TO SEGMENT BUSINESS MARKETS: A TEN-POINT PROGRAM

Will the segmentation study deliver the desired results—insightful market segments and workable, cost-effective strategies? A customized framework within which information can be gathered and analyzed is key to the process. Our two-part "game plan" consists of planning and research guidelines (see Box 3.1).[3]

Segmentation Planning

Sound planning gets the segmentation project off to a fast start. The first step is to set appropriate *segmentation objectives.* Careful problem definition is critical since it can overcome unintended outcomes such as incorrect research design, poor sampling, and/or meaningless or dangerous results.[4] A sample, but by no means exhaustive, list of questions relevant for analysis is provided in Box 3.2.

BOX 3.1. The Ten-Point Program for Conducting Segmentation Studies

Segmentation Planning Guidelines

1. Establish segmentation objectives
2. Specify target population measurement units
3. State relevant definitions
4. Recognize segmentation viability/segment formation criteria
5. Select segmentation bases

Segmentation Research Guidelines

6. Choose appropriate data collection methods
7. Employ sampling procedures
8. Analyze the data
9. Consider budgetary constraints
10. Know how the information will be used

BOX 3.2. Twenty Segmentation Objectives

1. What are some possible market segments/niches for your product or service?
2. How do these segments and market niches compare with your present customer profile(s)?
3. How large are these potential target markets?
4. What is the expected profitability of serving these submarkets?
5. How are these segments defined? (names, key variables)
6. What is unique about the specific groups?
7. Where are the potential customers located?
8. How much effort and resources should be allocated to the various market segments now? In the future?
9. What segments are competitors pursuing?
10. What competitive advantage does your company have compared to others in the market?
11. What past segmentation studies have been employed? How useful were past segmentation findings/strategies?
12. Who are the heavy users for your goods or services?
13. What features or benefits are sought by customers?
14. What alternative marketing strategies and tactics are available?
15. Does your product or service meet/exceed segment needs? (Any changes required?)
16. What promotional appeals can best be used toward the target markets?
17. How price sensitive are the markets?
18. What role do distribution channels play in the market?
19. How can the Internet be used to communicate with and serve your customers?
20. How will customer purchase behavior be measured and monitored to evaluate marketing effectiveness?

A two-stage approach to problem definition can be effective.[5] First, research objectives (ROs) are established. These provide a checklist of information needs useful for strategy development and may focus on segment identification, target market description, in-depth understanding of product usage, or validating market segments/niche opportunities. Second, a series of research questions (RQs) that relate to the focal problem statement is then developed, as shown in Box 3.3.

**BOX 3.3. A Segmentation Research Objective
and Research Questions
for an Automotive Services Study**

Research Objective

To determine the feasibility of WH Motors sponsoring a membership program for small business owners of leased or purchased vehicles including the postwarranty segment. The service package would consist of discounted auto/truck parts, routine and extended maintenance, repairs, paint, body work, short-term fleet increases, or other benefits sought by clients.

Research Questions

1. What are customer perceptions (reactions) and levels of interest, by segment, toward this program?
2. What specific features of the program are most and least attractive to new and existing buyers/lessees of WH Motors' vehicles?
3. What is an acceptable price for this membership program? Considerations include customer price expectations, price-level thresholds, cost-benefit trade-offs to WH Motors, and competitive offerings.
4. Who is the "typical customer" for this program based on firmographics, behavioral dimensions, and vehicle usage factors?
5. What are present purchasing habits of WH Motors' buyers for parts, accessories, maintenance, repairs, etc.?

In analyzing markets, we must operationalize and quantify the *target population measurement units*. Examples might include buyers, clients, customers, decision makers, influencers, lead users, managers, patients, prescreened prospects, purchasing agents, "tryers," etc. Once basic descriptors have been set, additional modifiers are needed to deal with multiple buying influences, decision-making units (DMUs), and buying centers.

In addition to customer specification, other *relevant definitions* are important in segmentation planning. The market service area is a critical one; geographical limitations should be noted (see Chapter 4). Factors that may affect this market definition include the nature of the business, the products offered, the customer profile, competition, technology, distribution channels, e-business initiatives, globalization strategy, usage patterns, etc.

Defined markets (see Chapter 2) must be assessed as to *segmentation viability*. Positive responses to the following "Four R" questions suggest that market segmentation is recommended. A negative response to one or more of these questions means that a redefinition of the market is necessary. Evaluate your situation based on these pivotal criteria:

1. Can you objectively and subjectively **rank** (prioritize) your target markets by their importance to your overall marketing program?
2. Are your target and niche markets of **realistic size,** i.e., large enough to profitably pursue? (Avoid the temptation to over-segment—dividing the market into a multitude of minimarkets; this is extremely costly and generally an ineffective marketing strategy.)
3. Can you **reach** your customers easily through trade journals, industrial directories, mailing lists, the Internet, or other media?
4. Will targeted customers **respond** to marketing initiatives?

Segment formation criteria include homogeneity within the segment (the test for similarities among group members), heterogeneity among segments (the test for differences among the various market segments), and meaningful segment data (practical, usable, and readily translatable into marketing strategy).

Markets can be segmented in many ways. There is no one clear, best method; a lot depends on a company's market situation and information needed by management. *Segmentation bases* are dimensions for segmenting a market and, in most cases, several of them will need to be considered simultaneously to provide a complete customer profile.

A useful dichotomy for classification is physical attributes (which are often readily observable) versus behavioral attributes (which are generally unobservable). Physical attributes regularly used in segmenting business markets include geographics; industrial classification codes

(NAICS/SIC); and firmographic factors such as years in business, size of the company, sales volume, etc. (Chapter 4). Behavioral attributes featured as business segmentation bases include product usage (Chapter 5), benefits (Chapter 6), and purchasing behavior and organizational psychographics (Chapter 7). Physical attributes are a priori variables (categories known in advance), while behavioral attributes may be both a priori, such as usage, or post hoc (segments determined after the analysis), such as benefits or psychographics.

A list of twenty segmentation bases frequently employed in B2B market situations is shown in Table 3.1.[6] How many of these approaches is your company currently using? Which of these approaches should your organization consider in your segmentation initiatives?

TABLE 3.1. Business Segmentation Bases

Type of Industry	Organizational Characteristics	Decision Makers (DMs)/Decision-Making Units (DMUs)	Product or Situational Variables
Industrial sectors— NAICS/SIC codes	Company size	Supplier loyalty	Technical requirements
End use, product application	Geographic location	Benefits derived from long-lasting relationships	Price sensitivity
	Purchasing volume	Personal background of DMs	Speed of delivery
	Purchasing frequency	Level of risk for a product purchase	Service quality required
	Purchasing situation	Seniority of DMs	Benefits derived from product use
	Corporate culture	Number of participants in the DMU	
		Roles of those in the DMU	

Source: Adapted from Stavros P. Kalafatis and Markos H. Tsogas, "Business Segmentation Bases: Congruence and Perceived Effectiveness," *Journal of Segmentation in Marketing,* 2(1), 1998, pp. 35-63.

Segmentation Research

A good segmentation study is built on objective, workable marketing information. Five *data collection methods* are vital to this process. Marketers can tap

1. published secondary research (data gathered for a purpose other than your current project),
2. primary research (quantitative or qualitative information collected for your project),
3. syndicated research (shared, purchased information),
4. database information (customer files), and
5. Internet sources (see Chapter 3 appendix).

Since secondary data offer tremendous cost and time savings over primary research, this information should be incorporated into your segmentation project, wherever feasible. Although data manipulation may be required, and publication lags and inappropriate measurement or classification units may be encountered, secondary research is a logical starting point for a segmentation study. As an example, trade associations and reference sources such as the *Market Share Reporter* or *Standard and Poor's Industry Surveys* can be very helpful in determining the size of the market, major competitors, and other basic industry information.

Secondary information was used as one determinant of the feasibility of establishing a battery (automobile, truck, and industrial) assembling plant in South Florida. Data supplied by the Independent Battery Manufacturers Association and the Battery Council International included such valuable references as statistics annuals, convention proceedings, and *The Battery Man* (a trade journal). Table 3.2 summarizes the major sources of secondary information useful for segmenting business markets.

Although secondary sources are important for solving "pieces of the puzzle," primary data are required to provide the balance of the marketing information that management needs. If you were seeking information on customers' perceptions about your product, a primary research approach would be required. Secondary data would be of limited help in

TABLE 3.2. Secondary Sources of Business Segmentation Information

Category	References
Business censuses (U.S. Government, <www.census.gov>)	Business Census Reports (Retail Trade, Wholesale Trade, Services, Construction, Manufacturing, Mineral Industries, and Transporation), *County Business Patterns*
Business demographics	*Demographics USA, Dun's Census of American Business, Editor & Publisher Market Guide,* Hoovers Handbooks, *Manufacturing & Distribution USA, Markets of the U.S. for Business Planners*
Business research databases/indexes (see *Gale Directory of Databases*)	ABI Inform, Business and Company Resource Center, Business and Industry, Dialog, General Business File ASAP, Mergent Online, Newspaper Abstracts, News Bank News File, New York Times Index, LexisNexis, Predicasts' Series, UMI's Newspaper Abstracts, US Industry and Trade Outlook, Wall Street Journal Index, Wilson Business Full Text (formerly known as Business Periodicals Index)
Directories	Directories in Print, Dun & Bradstreet Directories, *Encyclopedia of Associations, Findex Directory of Marketing Research Reports, Info USA, LexisNexis Corporate Affiliations, MacRAE's Blue Book, National Trade and Professional Associations of the U.S.,* State Industrial Directories, *Thomas Register, Ward's Business Directory of U.S. Private and Public Companies, Standard and Poor's Directories*
Statistical sources	Ameristat, *Market Share Reporter,* Predicasts Forecasts, Statistical Abstracts (U.S./states), *Standard and Poor's Industry Surveys,* TableBase, U.S. Department of Commerce Publications
Trade journals (includes special issues)	*Gale Directory of Publications and Broadcast Media, Harfax Guide to Industry Special Issues, Publicity Checker (Bacon's), Sales and Marketing Management's Survey of Buying Power, Special Issues Index by Greenwood Press, Standard Rate and Data Service—Business Publications and Data, Ulrich's International Periodicals Directory, Writer's Market, Gale Directory of Publications*

Source: Prepared by Art Weinstein. Research assistance provided by Dean Vellenga, Reference Librarian, Nova Southeastern University, April 2003.

Note: Although this table lists a lot of specific information (secondary) sources valuable for business market segmentation, in many cases additional legwork is required. For example, you can consult trade journal references to determine relevant publications in your industry. Then you will need to obtain these sources. Similarly, business indexes can be quite helpful for locating particular citations or abstracts, but you then must research specific articles to collect the information you need. Also, realize that some of these sources are likely to change over time (e.g., as to their name, coverage, format, or even availability), and new sources are always entering the marketing information field—astute analysts should be on the alert for these.

answering such a specific question. For most segmentation studies, primary research obtained via face-to-face meetings, telephone, direct mail, faxes, e-mail/Web sites, and/or focus groups will be the major source of marketing information. Behavioral segmentation dimensions such as adopter categories, benefits, and usage require customized research projects for given situations. Even firmographics that are readily available from secondary sources frequently need updated market measures, projections, and detailed analyses to maximize their value.

Secondary sources generally will solve part of the problem, and primary research is complex and costly. Syndicated or standardized information/services is an alternative or middle ground This hybrid approach, a cross between primary and secondary sources, can be of great value in complementing a firm's information needs at fees considerably below custom research projects. Essentially, syndicated research is cooperative information. Two or more companies are purchasing related information from a common research supplier.

Low-cost syndicated research reports ranging from a few hundred to many thousands of dollars are available for a multiplicity of industry sectors from dozens of companies, such as Dun & Bradstreet, FIND/SVP, and MarketResearch.com. For example, Market Research. com offers more than 40,000 publications from over 350 leading research firms.[7] Their *Findex 2002—The Definitive Global Market Research Directory* is a particularly strong resource. The following are four other leading syndicated research providers and some of their specialties:

- BizMiner—area profiles, high-growth firms, industry financial profiles
- Dataquest—computers, electronics, information technologies
- Frost & Sullivan—medical devices, military equipment, telecommunications
- J.D. Power and Associates—automobiles, energy, financials

While syndicated studies, reports, and surveys are highly useful, realize that, in isolation, the information provided is generally insufficient for effective segmentation. Additional primary, secondary, database, or Web sources are needed to present the total picture. An additional shortcoming of syndicated sources are that they are generic and market driven, as opposed to company and customer specific.

A recent development in segmentation research is database marketing, which is also called integrated marketing, relationship marketing, and single-source data by industry experts. This powerhouse technology is defined in detail:

> Managing a computerized relational database system, in real time, of comprehensive, up-to-date, relevant data on customers, inquiries, prospects, and suspects, to identify your most responsive customers for the purpose of developing a high-quality, long-standing relationship of repeat business, by developing predictive models which enable us to send desired messages at the right time in the right form to the right people—all with the result of pleasing our customers, increasing our response rate per marketing dollar, lowering our cost per order, building our business, and increasing our profits.[8]

This computer-driven approach measures marketing performance (e.g., sales, product usage, promotional effectiveness, etc.) via databases, electronic applications (e.g., advertising/couponing, frequency programs, scanners), factory shipments, etc. A tremendous amount of individualized customer data is generated, making segment-of-one marketing a viable option. Improvements in information technology allow marketers to create and sort ever-expanding databases. The key is to properly manage customer records and use this information effectively.

Tracking changing customer patterns over time—longitudinal analysis—is an important benefit of database technology. This has important implications for customer retention, customer upgrading, promotional activity, and competitive strategy.

Be cognizant of some shortcomings of databases, however. First, customer behavior is not explained; the data are quantitative and voluminous (this can easily lead to data overload) and do not qualitatively probe why customers act as they do. Databases are only partially useful in segmentation since they are data driven not strategic.

Second, some customers may be concerned about an invasion of privacy. Finally, there is the high cost of developing, implementing, and monitoring computer databases. These issues must be carefully weighed with respect to potential benefits.

Sampling procedures provide a cost-effective, realistic profile of a market. Major considerations include the segmentation sampling frame (the master listing of population elements), alternative sampling techniques (e.g., convenience, judgment, quota, random, systematic, snowball, stratified, and cluster samples), and the sample size.

It is presumed that the sampling frame is similar to the total population under study. For example, the CorpTech Directory of Technology Companies provides detailed information (contacts, SIC codes, business descriptions, annual sales) on more than 49,000 U.S.-based, high-tech manufacturers representing thousands of product categories in eighteen major industry groups.[9] This database/mailing list was found to be an excellent source for reaching top-ranking marketing executives in industrial high-technology markets.

There are two broad sampling categories to choose from: nonprobability or probability samples. Nonprobabilistic samples are the simplest and least expensive to use. These include convenience (participation is based on ease of access), judgment (expert opinions), and quota samples (key characteristics are intentionally matched to those of the population). The other set of options is probabilistic samples, which are more objective, difficult to administer, and costly than the former group. Cost, pragmatics, and time pressures often lead business marketers to choose nonprobabilistic sampling methods since they are easier to execute. While less than ideal from a methodological perspective, they are frequently "good enough" from a managerial perspective to collect valuable marketing information.

The size of the ideal sample is difficult to specify and depends on several factors. Among these are the type of sampling techniques selected; the data analysis approach used; the population characteristics; the importance of the decision; and the time, budget, and skills of marketing researchers available for the study. A review of past research initiatives conducted by the firm can also be quite helpful in this decision. I have seen research studies with very small samples (in-depth interviews of physicians, $n = 27$) provide tremendous segmentation insights while other projects that had 2,000 respondents were of limited value to management.

Data analysis begins before the segmentation data are collected. Have a clear understanding of what information is being sought. Dummy (blank data) tables can provide a research model for the analysis. Coding, cross-tabulations, and statistical computations—spanning the gamut from basic analysis (measures of central tendency and variability) to multivariate techniques (see Box 3.4)—are central at this stage. The goal is to assess the relationships between and among the key marketing variables.

BOX 3.4. Multivariate Statistical Techniques

The following synopsis provides a nontechnical overview of analytical techniques frequently employed in segmentation studies. These techniques are valuable when used in the right situation by experienced researchers. However, they should generally be used only once a basic understanding of a market exists. In this capacity, they can be very helpful for enhancing and complementing prior segmentation findings. The objective of this summary is not to explain how to use multivariate analysis (that is a book in itself), but rather to acquaint the marketing planner with potential applications for these procedures. Just as carpenters carry many tools in their toolbox, the segmentation researcher should be knowledgeable about various analytical procedures. Interested readers are advised to consult marketing research or statistics texts for further information on multivariate statistical techniques. Two very good sources are by Churchill[a] and Hair et al.[b] Here are eight major multivariate options for B2B segmentation.

CHAID (Chi-Square Automatic Interaction Detection)

CHAID is the most common of all tree classifiers. CHAID categorizes all independent continuous and multivalued integer variables by "similarity measures" and considers the resulting categories for a variable as a whole unit (group) for splitting purposes.[c]

Cluster Analysis

Under this procedure, a set of related objects or variables (e.g., geodemographic or psychographic) is analyzed, and through grouping techniques, segments are formed that have similarities in the overall statistical measure and are therefore likely to exhibit similar purchasing behavior.

Conjoint Analysis

Also called multiple trade-off analysis, this analytical method measures the impact of varying product attribute mixes on the purchase decision. It models customer preferences or reactions to product concepts in terms of bundles of attributes. This statistical approach ranks customer perceptions and preferences toward products. These are then evaluated and grouped for segment homogeneity. Conjoint measurement is frequently used for new product design, pricing value studies, vendor/competitor evaluation, and media selection.

Discriminant Analysis

This technique is useful for comparing differences between segments or predicting group membership. Discriminant analysis is performed through computer-generated equations (discriminant functions). This technique is effective in profiling Japanese versus American buyers, heavy versus light users, loyal versus nonloyal customers, or adopters versus nonadopters for a new product concept, to show a few applications.

Factor Analysis

Factor analysis is a marketing research technique that analyzes a large number of variables and reduces them to a smaller number of key factors to better explain a given marketing situation. Factor analysis is useful in benefit and psychographic research segmentation. There are two major types of factor analyses used in market segmentation studies. R-factor analysis reduces the amount of data by finding similarities in responses to particular variables. Q-factor analysis (the more important customer segmenting means) finds groupings of people who respond similarly to research issues.

(continued)

(continued)

Multidimensional Scaling

Also referred to as perceptual mapping, this analytical technique graphically represents product attributes based on customers' perceptions and preferences for brands, product or service categories, and/or ideal products. The objective of multidimensional scaling is to identify market segments of customers with similar needs or attitudes toward products. Since more than two attributes cannot be visually depicted in two-dimensional space, variables are computer reduced to portray appropriate market measures. This technique is frequently used in benefit and perceptual segmentation studies.

Multiple Regression

This versatile research technique is useful in analyzing associations among marketing variables. A mathematical equation is derived measuring a single dependent (criterion) variable based on two or more independent (predictor or explanatory) variables. Predicting product usage as a function of years in business and revenues is an example of regression.

Structural Equation Modeling

This is a causal modeling approach that explains relationships among a set of manifest (observed) variables in terms of latent (unobserved) variables.[d] This approach was used for testing competitive intensity, market and technological orientation, and their impact on market definition success in industrial high-technology markets.

[a]Gilbert A. Churchill Jr., *Marketing Research: Methodological Foundations,* Sixth Edition (Fort Worth, TX: Dryden, 1994).

[b]Joseph F. Hair Jr., Ralph E. Anderson, and Ronald L. Tatham, *Multivariate Data Analysis with Readings,* Second Edition (New York: Macmillan Publishers, 1987).

[c]Nissan Levin and Jacob Zahavi, "Predictive Modeling Using Segmentation," *Journal of Interactive Marketing,* 15(2), 2001, pp. 18-19.

[d]J. Scott Long, "Confirmatory Factor Analysis: A Preface to LISREL," *Sage University Paper Series on Quantitative Applications in the Social Sciences,* 07-033 (Beverly Hills: Sage Publications, 1983).

In data analysis, practicality is of the essence. A complex segmentation model is not advisable if a simpler design adequately provides the required information. Statistical software packages such as SPSS and SAS are being used frequently by marketers to analyze a wide range of segmentation research problems. For secondary research, analysis often means updating and verifying information, manipulating figures, and adapting the data to appropriate units of measure for a given study.

Management is always concerned about *budgetary constraints*. In many cases, a hybrid approach is desirable. The company may have the resources to assist in the segmentation analysis, but consultants can design the research plan, oversee the data collection process, and/or analyze the data. This is particularly useful when confronted by a complex methodology such as benefit segmentation. Also, consider the expected value of the information. A $100,000 research project should not be authorized if it is likely to produce only $75,000 worth of answers.

The final research element, *know how the information will be used,* relates directly to the first planning guideline *(establish research objectives)*. Carefully prepared objectives provide you with clues to many of the answers to questions asked by management. New knowledge, serendipity, or surprising statistics are not important unless they are useful for marketing planning, strategy, or control. Written reports are seldom sufficient. Market research briefings that incorporate multimedia presentations, segmentation summaries, and lots of Q&A (questions and answers) are recommended for conveying technical information and segmentation recommendations to management.

Another consideration is the "real" purpose of the study. Research is sometimes authorized in order to justify a preconceived opinion, attitude, or position held on a subject by management. In such an instance, unless the findings agree with the established notion, the results of the research project will be downplayed or ignored.

Marketing information serves a definite purpose in the business world. It reduces uncertainty and provides a knowledge base upon which marketing decisions can be made. Segmentation SkillBuilder 3 captures the key planning and research issues that need to be addressed in the design and execution of a successful segmentation

SEGMENTATION SKILLBUILDER 3:
DESIGNING THE SEGMENTATION STUDY

You are the Market Segmentation Manager for your company and your input is solicited for developing next year's marketing plan. Reviewing your research needs, you note the need for a major segmentation analysis for an important product or product line.

1. Explain the background situation and need for this study to your company's Vice President of Marketing (note: you will likely have to sell this project, internally).

2. The VP likes your concept (#1) and is thinking about moving forward with this project. She asks you to flesh out some planning and methodological details regarding the segmentation project. Comment on the following issues:

   a. Research design—exploratory, descriptive, or causal

   b. Data sources—primary, secondary, syndicated, database, or Web

   c. Segmentation dimensions—physical or behavioral and types (primary and secondary bases)

   d. Survey instrument/approach to be used—questionnaire (type), focus group, observation form, etc.; field procedures and controls

   e. Sampling plan—probability or nonprobability sample (type); sample size

   f. Analytical and statistical methods

   g. Personnel, time frame, budgeted investment, and projected value of the study.

3. How would you explain your research needs to an outside marketing research/consulting firm? Develop the specific objectives of a proposed study and associated research questions based on the objectives (see the earlier discussion of segmentation planning in the section Using Planning and Research to Segment Business Markets and review Boxes 3.1 through 3.3).

study. The bottom line is that the information must be practical, workable, and utilized. Business Segmentation Insight 3 clarifies the segmentation research challenge.

BUSINESS SEGMENTATION INSIGHT 3:
SEGMENTATION RESEARCH—AN ASSESSMENT

The research approach a firm uses depends greatly on the stage of segmentation analysis that the firm is in. For example, if a company has never formally analyzed the marketplace to derive potential target segments, exploratory research is recommended. The purpose of this research is to obtain as much market information that may be relevant to the situation as possible. Since precise information needs are indeterminable at this stage, secondary sources will play a prominent role in the research.

Complex segmentation analyses are seldom advisable for initial studies or ones using new segmentation bases and variables. At this juncture, the challenge is to focus on customers as people rather than undertaking a number-crunching exercise. Explore customer characteristics, needs, and wants and design marketing strategies to best serve your preliminary target markets.

As the market information is sifted through and a better understanding of basic relationships becomes evident, primary research projects can be undertaken. At the other extreme is the well-versed company that has defined and described the market in terms of segment profiles through firmographics, product usage criteria, and purchasing factors. A need for a higher-level segmentation analysis may become evident. A causality design (such as benefit segmentation) can be introduced, whereby purchase behavior is linked to isolated variables.

Once an in-depth understanding of a market situation exists, advanced methodologies make sense. Cluster and factor analyses, multidimensional scaling, and other multivariate statistical techniques (e.g., CHAID, multiple regression, structural equation modeling, etc.) can be quite insightful if used in the right situations by skilled researchers.

Segmentation research can take many forms. It can vary from an initial full-blown or baseline study to an investigation into one or more aspects of a market. Some compromises may often be necessary, recognizing the company's research needs and budgetary constraints.

Ongoing or periodic studies should also be planned, given the dynamic nature of markets. The bottom line is that a company should use whatever source of information that can best meet its needs at a cost it can afford. Typically, this will mean multiple sources—secondary, primary, syndicated, databases, and/or the Internet. This research can either be conducted in-house through the marketing research department or contracted to a commercial marketing research firm or marketing consultant. Talk to industry experts or visit the American Marketing Association's Web site (www. marketingpower.com or www.quirks.com) for guidance in selecting companies capable of doing segmentation projects.

In addition, universities can be of great value in designing and/or implementing segmentation studies. Many universities have research bureaus, specialized business centers, or Small Business Institutes that can provide advice and technical assistance for such projects. Of course, marketing faculty can also be an excellent source for obtaining consultants specializing in segmentation analysis.

As Table 3.3 explains, scholars and practitioners have different expectations as to the value of market segmentation. While on the surface it appears that we have two competing target markets, this does not have to be the case. Knowledge transfer and collaboration between both factions should be highly encouraged. As a professor/consultant with one foot in the "ivory tower" and the other in the "real-world trenches," I have found that good segmentation research and thinking comes from both perspectives. In fact, each group can greatly benefit from what the other brings to the table in terms of expertise, experience, and objectivity.[10] Consider and profit from this duality as you read the material on market segmentation that follows.

Although at times it can be costly, research should be a high priority in a firm's marketing budget. The alternative to research is trial and error. Can your company afford the cost of failure through guesswork? The cost of "missing the boat" is often much greater than the cost of solid information. Marketing research can be thought of as a high-yielding cash value insurance policy. It can protect the company from marketing mistakes but also return great dividends through identifying potential new opportunities. Market research facilitates executive decision making. Raphael and Parket offer five solid recommendations for marketing managers:

1. Market research should be proactive, not reactive.
2. Bring in market research early in the decision process.

3. Product teams should include a representative from market research.
4. Develop corporate policies requiring managers to utilize market research.
5. Give market research a direct line to upper management.[11]

Most of the time (my estimate is about 98 percent), research-based answers are possible in segmentation situations. The "hit list" approach is a useful technique for conducting this research. Develop a list of the six to ten issues that come to mind immediately as research needs. Ask a key associate or two to add to this list and let your right brain (creative side) take over this task for a couple of days. The expanded list may now contain twelve to twenty items. From my experience, it is likely that you can find about two-thirds of your answers from secondary, syndicated, or Internet sources. Primary research and databases should account for most of the balance. Sometimes (in about 2 percent of the cases), however, research is not the way to go; i.e., it is too costly to solve the problem or research cannot effectively solve the problem. Hence, management insight may provide us with the appropriate solution.

Despite the inherent value of research, there is still a place for "gut feeling" in the business environment. Top executives know that the "judgment call" may at times be the difference between what works

TABLE 3.3. The Value of Segmentation Research—Two Views

Segmentation Issue	Academic Concerns	Practitioner Concerns
Purpose of the study	Intellectual curiosity, develop/refine research techniques, find new industry applications	Solve marketing problems, make sound customer-related decisions
Objective/desired outcome	Advance state-of-the-art, get published	Increase sales, increase market share, enhance customer retention rate
Research basis	Rigor with some relevance	Relevance—rigor if relevant
Theory basis	Relatively important	Relatively unimportant—important only if theory assists in accomplishing stated objectives

and what does not. Although Japanese companies use quantitative surveys, primarily, they rely on their instincts. Their soft or qualitative research often includes observing customers in their natural environments and in-depth talks with marketing channel members. Creative and winning strategies are often the end result.

Intuition and analysis offer a logical basis for building first-draft segmentation representations. The collective experience and expertise of marketers offers great insights on customer needs, product preferences, buying patterns, and related segmenting dimensions. Paul Millier illustrates this process for a new aluminum alloy aimed at the automotive industry. He concludes that intuitive knowledge yields highly testable segmentation matrices and this is a valuable starting point for subsequent refinement.[12]

SUMMARY

The success of your market segmentation program is dependent on the planning and research process employed in designing, collecting, and analyzing relevant customer information. Segmentation analysis must be practical to be effective. This can be accomplished by utilizing systematic planning frameworks, soliciting the involvement of management at all levels within the company, and using appropriate analytical methods. The result of such efforts will be segmentation findings that are readily translated into marketing strategy; ultimately, this will improve business performance. A ten-point program for designing a good market segmentation study was introduced. Five planning guidelines and five research guidelines were discussed in this chapter. Chapter 4 considers geographics and firmographics.

APPENDIX: INTERNET SEGMENTATION— BUSINESS MARKETING APPLICATIONS

Two of the most interesting and useful aspects of the Internet marketplace are providing research and targeting specific marketing segments. A

This appendix was extracted from an article by Susie Chang, "Internet Segmentation: State-of-the-Art Marketing Applications," *Journal of Segmentation in Marketing*, 2(1), 1998, pp. 19-34, and is reprinted with permission of The Haworth Press, Inc. At the time of the writing, she was Business Analyst, Oracle Corporation, Redwood Shores, California.

plethora of free information on Net users and their habits exists on the Web. In addition, marketers can conduct their own online research inexpensively through e-mail and a variety of Web site analysis tools. Target marketing on the Web means customizing content and advertising for each individual user. This briefing explains how to use this twenty-first-century medium effectively, today.

Since the introduction of the World Wide Web in 1991, use of the Internet has grown faster than any other electronic medium, including the telegraph. Growth of the Internet (popularly known as the "Net") has been significantly influenced by a number of new technological developments and marketplace factors. Commercial uses have witnessed the most dramatic increase. The exponential increase in Net users and electronic commerce during the preceding several years demonstrates that the Internet and the World Wide Web (known popularly by its three-letter initialism, WWW, as well as its abbreviated form, the "Web") are media that marketers cannot afford to ignore. The Internet attracts a sophisticated consumer who demands timely information and personalized service. It also attracts businesses that are responsive to customer needs and the changing marketplace.

The interactive nature of the Internet provides several benefits to marketers and consumers that traditional media do not. Chief among these is the ability to effectively segment and target markets. Net users are far from a homogenous group: in fact, they delight in their heterogeneity. An ever-changing online world composed of diverse individuals and organizations affords them the opportunity to escape mass-marketed, mass-produced products, services, and ideas. The Internet is so successful and revolutionary as a marketing medium because it offers (1) up-to-the-minute information for sellers and buyers, (2) a less expensive and more expansive form of advertising and distribution, (3) customization of advertising and services, and (4) the ability for businesses to track the success of marketing practices.

Determining Market Segments

The Internet Marketplace has the ability to assist marketers in gathering accurate market research. Online market research is, of course, essential to online marketing and selling efforts but it can also be valuable to offline marketing campaigns. Research can be conducted in a variety of ways. Marketers can search the Web for free surveys or purchase research from professional firms. Organizations that maintain a Web site can examine usage logs or conduct private research through the use of cookies (see www. cookiecentral.com) and opt-in advertising.

A plethora of free information on Net users and their habits is available on the Web. Many Internet market research firms, such as Nua Internet Consultancy and Developer (www.nua.ie), CyberAtlas (www.cyberatlas.com), and GVU User Surveys (www.gvu.gatech.edu), make their findings available at no charge. Nua's site, in particular, is an excellent site for research, as it indexes studies from many firms on a variety of topics. The site is also searchable and includes links to primary syndicated research firms such as Forrester (www.forrester.com), Jupiter Communications (www.jup.com), Gartner Group (www.gartner.com), International Data Corporation (www. idcresearch.com), CommerceNet/Nielsen (www.commerce.net), and advantage (www.advantage.com). These organizations make most of their studies available for relatively high fees but often they offer executive summaries for free or nominal-fee downloads.

These firms also advertise customized market research services. Because cyberspace greatly reduces the difficulties of conducting business long-distance, the Internet exposes marketers to a wider choice of firms that might be available within an organization's geographic region. In addition, marketers can purchase demographic and psychographic information from other content providers. Content providers may then make their registration and user preference lists available to third parties. (*Note:* a great deal of controversy surrounds access to user data by third parties.) Ethically created and distributed lists contain highly reliable prospects because users prequalify themselves by visiting sites related to a marketer's product and by "opting in" to receive third-party solicitations. Registered users may also specify in what way they would like to receive information—via e-mail, telephone, or postal mail.

In addition to the wealth of research available from outside sources, marketers can conduct their own online research inexpensively through Web sites, e-mail, and a variety of Web site analysis tools. Surveys, for example, are easy to administer through a link on an existing site, through dedicated sites, or through e-mail. In exchange for a free sample of a product, service, or timely information, users will answer a questionnaire, especially if they believe their participation will improve the services they receive. This is also true of registration and/or access fees for specific site content. Users are more inclined to take the time to register a username and password, if they receive a tangible benefit from doing so.

Businesses can also infer user psychographics from server logs and cookies by analyzing the time spent at a site or particular Web page, the last site the user visited, or keywords that the user inputs to navigate to and through a Web site. Furthermore, marketers can take advantage of studies conducted by research firms advertising their services on the Web, often making their findings available through Web downloads.

All of this information helps sellers segment their market according to geographic region, affinity, age, income, benefits sought, family size, and lifestyle. What distinguishes online market segmentation research from traditional research methods is the timeliness of the information and the Web's worldwide reach. State-of-the-art technology allows Web site content providers to continuously monitor customer activity and immediately respond. The low cost of Internet connections and Net applications, together with the growing popularity of the Internet outside the United States, enables organizations to research potential markets across the world.

Target Marketing Implications

The interactive nature of the Net makes it a prime medium for marketing to specific target segments. This is especially true for information-rich products and services. Companies that provide timely and relevant information to their clients, while only subtly marketing to them, will realize the most success with electronic commerce. Successful sites will offer facts, news, knowledge, and advice. They will also allow users to customize every aspect of their experiences, from the advertising banners they see to the interest-specific content. Target marketing on the Web means customizing content for each individual user—not just for a community of users.

Electronic newsletters, often referred to as e-zines or discussion lists, are moderated forums for exchanges of ideas by sellers, clients, competitors, and other interested parties. They are highly targeted, due to the fact that users must "subscribe" to receive a newsletter by e-mail. Although e-zines, newsletters, and discussion lists are slightly different, they each direct targeted information to subscribers. Most lists permit only the moderator and those who subscribe to post comments. Newsletters are effective promotion because they continually place the marketer's name before a group of largely qualified, interested parties. E-zines provide timely, useful information on new developments, successes and failures with a product or service, as well as answers to frequently asked questions. Marketers can use their list of newsletter subscribers and the feedback they receive in the list discussions to conduct additional online and offline marketing.

Another method to target segments is to sponsor Internet content. Marketers can sponsor related Web sites, newsletters, and contests. Sponsorship supports relevant content on the Internet without intrusive advertising messages. Sponsors also reach highly targeted prospects by linking their names with related products, services, and concepts.

A method to target segments based on geographic location and/or product category is to participate in a regional or industry-specific Web mall. As the Web becomes more crowded, marketers are finding that one of the best strategies to bring visitors to their sites is to link the site to a specialized Web mall. These cooperative sites are particularly popular in the manufacturing industry and among "communities of users" defined by a common interest or background, such as region, or product ownership. The idea is applicable to any industry. Users can quickly find news, company listings, and discussion groups, as well as purchase goods and services. In addition, regionally specific sites attract Internet users whose commonality is their location. Content providers can sponsor a cybermall, purchase advertising banners, or link their corporate sites to the mall through hypertext. The advantages of a Web mall or electronic plaza are a highly concentrated target market and shared costs for a Web presence.

Finally, the most effective and the most technologically advanced method of target marketing is customizable Web sites. These sites require user registration and user profiles to display personalized content. Personalized Web content makes possible target marketing to audiences of one. Cookies, CGI (common gateway interface) scripts, and Java applets remember demographic and psychographic information such as user passwords, credit card numbers, keywords, products owned, and so on. CGI scripts and Java applets are code inserted in an HTML document that enables Web servers to run and interact with external applications stored elsewhere on the remote system or network.

PART II:
BUSINESS SEGMENTATION BASES

Chapter 4

Geographics and Firmographics

Segmentation by demographic characteristics of both businesses and the marketplace is relatively easy, quite useful, and inexpensive. And when combined with traditional segmentation factors such as product use, demographic data provide a much clearer view of the market. Segmentation using demographic information in the early stages of market development allows managers to be proactive.

Rodney L. Griffith and Louis G. Pol (1994)

Marketers should evaluate a myriad of descriptive characteristics when identifying and selecting business market segments. These critical issues can be understood by analyzing geodemographic attributes or firmographics. These segmentation bases provide important decision-oriented insights about high-tech, industrial, and service markets. Geodemographic segmentation is a logical starting point because (1) the data are obtainable through secondary sources, government agencies, or demographic vendors; (2) it provides a quick snapshot of a market—an understanding of market structure and potential customer segments; and (3) target populations can be sampled to represent characteristics of the entire market at a much lower cost than other forms of business segmentation.

Wind and Cardoza advocate a two-stage approach to industrial segmentation that consists of macrosegments and microsegments.[1] They explain that macrosegments consist of key organizational characteristics such as size of the buying firm, SIC (Standard Industrial Classification) category, geographic location, and usage factors (see Chapter 5). In some cases, single-stage segmentation based primarily on business demographics is sufficient for identifying and targeting markets. More typical, however, is that a two-stage approach that will employ benefits (see Chapter 6) and organizational psychographics and purchasing criteria (see Chapter 7) will be needed to provide complete market profiles.

Firmographic segmentation begins with geographic factors. Geographic analysis is one of the simplest methods for dividing markets into possible target segments. Regional differences can greatly impact purchasing behavior and product consumption. Geographic segmentation bases, market area definition, and using the Census Bureau's business information products are the key issues discussed in the first part of this chapter.

Major business demographic variables—i.e., age of the firm and stage of the product life cycle, financial factors, market size, (business) ownership factors, and industry structure—are the focus of the second part of the chapter. Due to their strategic importance in business segmentation, particular attention is paid to two industry structure/business type classifications: NAICS (North American Industrial Classification System) codes and NACE, a European taxonomy.

GEOGRAPHIC SEGMENTATION BASES

There is no single, best method for geographically segmenting the market. Factors to consider include the market you are competing in, available corporate resources (assets, capital, personnel, and technology), competitors' strategies, flexibility in the manipulation of the marketing mix variables, and the firm's operating philosophy. Major geographic segmentation dimensions can be grouped into two categories, market scope factors and geographic market measures, as follows.

Market Scope

Global Scope

Is your marketing strategy designed to be worldwide, international regional (e.g., Latin America or Asia), selected countries (e.g., Canada or United Kingdom), or domestic market only? An interesting view of North America stated that there were "nine nations" rather than three. These nations (and their capital cities) were Islands (Miami), Empty Quarter (Denver), Breadbasket (Kansas City), Quebec (Quebec City), New England (Boston), Dixie (Atlanta), Ecotopia (San Francisco), Mexamerica (Los Angeles), and Foundry (Detroit).[2]

Many high-tech and industrial firms organize their marketing and sales efforts by worldwide regions. In addition to the usual North American, European, Asia Pacific, and Latin American divisions, companies such as Bayer use an ROW ("rest of the world") designation to refer to other international market opportunities.

National/Regional Scope

Within the United States, companies may go after the entire country, regional markets (Southeast or Pacific Northwest), states, or metropolitan areas. Non-American companies also have similar options available (e.g., Western Canada; French-speaking Quebec province; major cities such as Calgary, Montreal, Toronto, Vancouver, etc.).

Local Scope

Local markets include counties, cities, townships, ZIP codes, and/ or neighborhoods. As an example, New South Construction Co. has grown from $4 million in revenues in 1990 to $65 million a decade later by focusing on airport projects, corporate work, private schools, private clubs, and industrial office buildings in and around the Atlanta area.[3]

Geographic Market Measures

Census Classifications

Metropolitan Statistical Areas (MSAs), Primary Metropolitan Statistical Areas (PMSAs), and Consolidated Metropolitan Statistical Areas (CMSAs) are some of the more important geographic breakdowns U.S. marketers need to be familiar with (see Box 4.1 for a further discussion of U.S. Census classifications).

From 1990 to 2000, the five fastest-growing states were all located in the West: Nevada (66 percent), Arizona (40 percent), Colorado (31 percent), Utah (30 percent), and Idaho (29 percent). Overall, California registered the largest numeric increase—4.1 million people. Also, all ten of the fastest-growing metropolitan areas were found in the South and West.[4]

Standardized Market Area Measures

The use of standardized market areas is often a useful first-cut approach to segmentation. Leading marketing research companies have designated geographic market areas for media coverage and other

---

BOX 4.1. Census Geography

According to the Bureau of the Census, an area qualifies for recognition as a Metropolitan Statistical Area (MSA) in one of two ways: if it is a city with at least 50,000 inhabitants or an urbanized area with a total metropolitan population of at least 100,000 (75,000 in New England).

In addition to the county (the "central county") containing the largest city, an MSA also includes additional counties ("outlying counties") having strong economic and social ties to the central county, determined chiefly by the extent of the urbanized area and census data on commuting to work. An MSA may contain more than one city with a population of 50,000 and may cross state lines.

If an area has more than 1 million people and meets certain other specified requirements, it is termed a Consolidated Metropolitan Statistical Area (CMSA). This consists of major components called Primary Metropolitan Statistical Areas (PMSAs). As of June 30, 1999, there were eighteen CMSAs consisting of seventy-three PMSAs, and 258 defined MSAs in the fifty U.S. states (one CMSA, three PMSAs, and three MSAs may be found in Puerto Rico).

Source: U.S. Census Bureau, Population Division, Revised August 2, 2002. For further information contact Laura K. Yax at <www.census.gov/population/www/estimates/aboutmetro.html>.

studies. Arbitron's Areas of Dominant Influence (ADIs) and A.C. Nielsen's Designated Market Areas (DMAs) are two such examples. The thirty-two National Football League franchise cities represent an alternative schema for identifying large markets (with the exception of Green Bay, Wisconsin). Geographic market penetration indexes can be readily computed to compare specific markets to national averages.

Population Density and Climate-Related Factors

Urban, suburban, or rural markets reveal population density levels and other relevant market characteristics that relate to purchase behavior. Security devices are popular in inner cities, while rural markets are likely to purchase farm equipment.

Defining Market Areas

The market scope and geographic market measures provide a basic framework of the most common dimensions upon which geographic market decisions can be based. The categories are not mutually exclusive, however. Within some classifications, more than one variable should be examined, and several forms of geographic bases should be assessed to maximize the value of the marketing information. How do you define your market geographically? (You should review Segmentation Skillbuilder 4 as a starting point.)

A major strategic decision that all companies face is how to define and best serve their geographic market areas. Many options are possible, spanning the gamut from the global view (the multinational company) to the local view (the small business owner). As Business Segmentation Insight 4 explains, leading pharmaceutical firms frequently use geographic sales territories as a basis for segmenting markets.

To better understand their markets, business marketers can benefit by identifying a primary trade area (PTA) and secondary trade area (STA). Sometimes, even a tertiary trade area (TTA) is desirable. For example, an industrial pumps distributor based in Jacksonville, Florida, might define its market as primarily regional (65 percent of sales from the southeastern U.S. states—its PTA), 25 percent national (STA), and 10 percent international (TTA).

SEGMENTATION SKILLBUILDER 4:
DEFINING GEOGRAPHIC MARKETS

Using the geographic segmentation insights described in this chapter, how do you presently define your market? Are there other geographic approaches that you are not using but should use? Here are ten issues to ponder:

1. Do you compete internationally? (If not, go to question 3.)
2. Are your products marketed worldwide or to selected nations/regions? Specify current and proposed markets.
3. Are your products sold in two or more U.S. states? Specify current and proposed regions/states. (If you do business locally or in a single state, go to question 9.)
4. What CMSAs, PMSAs, and MSAs are you targeting now or thinking about targeting?
5. Are you using ADIs or DMAs to define markets?
6. Does population density (urban, suburban, or rural) impact your geographic market definition?
7. Does climate affect your geographic market definition?
8. How do regional factors impact your market?
9. Are your products sold locally? Specify current and proposed counties, cities, townships, and/or ZIP codes.
10. Have you identified primary, secondary, and/or tertiary trade areas?

BUSINESS SEGMENTATION INSIGHT 4:
HOW A MAJOR PHARMACEUTICAL COMPANY USES GEOGRAPHIC
SALES ANALYSIS TO SEGMENT ITS MARKETS

One would have to describe the segmentation approach at a major pharmaceutical company (MPC) as continually evolving. Originally, the entire basis of segmentation was that of geographic distinctions. The design was simply to overlay the number of available sales territories to the entire country proportional to the number of physicians in the target market in each area. This approach had the dual advantages of keeping sales force costs low (reduced travel) and an in-depth knowledge of the local marketing situation.

All physicians were not included in the geographic target market. The product portfolio determined the type of physician most likely to prescribe the products. Consequently, the typical territory included physicians in certain hospital departments, primary care physicians (pediatricians, family practice, internal medicine, and doctors of osteopathy), cardiologists, endocrinologists, and urologists. MPC could safely ignore the rest of the physician market and be relatively sure that the prime, most profitable segments of the market were being covered.

MPC began the process of dividing a portion of its sales force to call on important specialties that would likely attract comarketing partners. The advantage to MPC was that for little additional cost they could call on the same physicians and greatly enhance revenue and profitability. Therefore, they sequentially began to set up territories based on certain physician and hospital specialties. The first was the cardiology specialty group. Then they added endocrinology, and in a succession of years, other specialties were covered.

This segmentation strategy worked well. The additional revenue that these agreements brought into the company led to the idea that, perhaps, more money could be made by buying the originating companies outright (hence, a corporate acquisitions strategy was pursued). The sales force was now expanded by approximately one-third. Research by outside consultants found that it would be best to have each primary care sales force sell four (in some cases three) drugs, and then divisionalize the sales force. This resulted in nine divisions of MPC to call on primary care physicians. In addition to the primary care sales force, the specialty divisions were kept intact and expanded in size. This resulted in intensive coverage of the intended target market.

With the introduction of a comarketing agreement for a blockbuster drug product, MPC set up an allergy specialty sales force to call on allergists in their offices. An examination of the most profitable potential alignment revealed, however, that growth in this pharmaceutical category was limited by three key factors: (1) usage of prescription antihistamines was not growing as rapidly as had been anticipated, (2) the use of nasal sprays increased, and (3) the growing over-the-counter (OTC) market. At the same time, another class of drugs were rapidly expanding— COX-2 Inhibitors (used for arthritic symptoms, pain, and related syndromes). After examining the growth pattern of this market, it was decided to redeploy the allergy sales force to the COX-2 Inhibitor sales force. This redeployment meant the same resources could be allocated to a much faster-growing market. This repositioning supported two MPC products considered "stars" based on the Boston Consulting Group's strategic matrix, i.e., a large market share in a fast-growth market.

In addition to this segmentation by geography and specialty, MPC uses microsegmentation within each of these categories. The ability to sort physicians by any number of parameters has evolved to a fine degree. Sales representatives (and anyone else in the company for that matter, e.g., district managers and marketing managers in the regional and home offices) can simultaneously sort physicians in any territory (which is defined both geographically and by type of physician) according to these parameters: speed of adoption of new drugs in a particular class, use of managed care versus fee for service, amount of use in the drug class, amount of use of the MPC drug being considered, ZIP code, and amount of use of the drug category relative to all other doctors. Using an Excel spreadsheet with macros enabled, the sales representatives need only specify which parameter to sort by first, and then second and then third. Currently, the maximum is three simultaneous sorts. This sorting process is dynamic and new updates are continually arriving via electronic downloads to laptops. Consequently, the sales representative at MPC has the ability to maximize time with the physician-customers who have the potential and likelihood to dramatically increase sales and profits.

Source: Contributed by G. H., a sales manager with one of the world's largest pharmaceutical companies. He requested that his company name not be identified in this segmentation application, hence, the MPC designation.

TAPPING CENSUS PRODUCTS FOR GEOGRAPHICS AND BUSINESS DEMOGRAPHICS

It has often been said that the business world is a jungle. Perhaps that means that you need to add a TIGER to your side. The TIGER (Topologically Integrated Geographic Encoding and Referencing) system is one of the Census Bureau's newer and more innovative services; it provides computer-readable mapping and a geographic database on a statewide basis and for the entire United States. Plotting geographic coordinates, TIGER serves as the underlay for address/

area data (e.g., demographic, economic, etc.) that result in high-quality, digital maps.

Here are some marketing and geographic information system (GIS) applications for the TIGER system. Direct marketers and delivery-intensive businesses can greatly benefit from TIGER. For example, FedEx drivers can easily locate their targeted destinations to deliver faster. TIGER is also valuable for site selection decisions, analyzing trade areas, setting up distribution routes, tracking subscriber services, and targeted promotion (e.g., direct mailings). Future enhancements through the incorporation of demographics, behavioral approaches, and product usage data can make TIGER even stronger for market segmentation.

Since TIGER/Line files require further data processing, you might want to consider using a "TIGER trainer" (specialist) to generate your maps. Dozens of vendors, such as Claritas, a demographic leader, have the capacity to process TIGER files. For further information on the TIGER resource list and other relevant business census products, contact the U.S. Census Bureau (a division of the Department of Commerce) at (301) 763-INFO (4636), <www.census.gov>, or e-mail <tiger@census.gov>.

For example, the Census Bureau sells non-TIGER mapping products. Metropolitan area wall maps—great for plotting geographic sales territories and market penetration—are available for $16. A set of fifty-two metropolitan area page maps (8.5" × 11") for all the states plus the District of Columbia and Puerto Rico costs $25. These may be viewed online in PDF form via the Adobe Acrobat Reader.

Business Census products are disseminated every five years ending in 2 and 7 (1997, 2002, 2007, and so forth). Hundreds of reports are for sale in a variety of formats such as CD-ROM, diskette, DVD-ROM, and publications typically ranging from about $30 to $200 (most are about $50 or so). In addition to the Census Web site and phone number provided earlier, queries on materials about economic and business statistics can be directed to <econ@census.gov>. The Census Bureau also sponsors a series of seminars for businesspeople.

In addition, many demographic companies (consult the latest annual *American Demographics Marketing Tools Sourcebook* for a detailed list of leading industry suppliers) offer Census-based and other geodemographic products. Microsoft's bCentral.com Web site is a recent entrant in the online demographic data market, a sector dominated by Claritas, SRC, and MapInfo. As part of its niche marketing strategy, Microsoft views the 5 million American businesses with fifty or fewer employees as an attractive target market.[5]

County and state planning agencies can also provide useful maps and demographic information. A former small business client of mine obtained an armful of reports, maps, and statistical publications from the Miami–Dade County (Florida) Planning Department for under $50. This information was vital in making future strategic marketing decisions for his business with respect to site selection, market definition, segmentation, product mix, and promotion.

Also, let us not forget computer mapping, which has become a popular tool for market analysis. To get started in mapping, you need a quality PC, printer/plotter, cartographic database, demographic database, and software that links them together.[6] Box 4.2 lists ten im-

---

BOX 4.2. Computer Mapping: Key Questions

1. What type of system is appropriate: PC-based, mini, or mainframe?
2. What type of software is provided?
3. How good is the quality of the finished maps?
4. Are zooming (the ability to blow up the picture) capabilities provided?
5. Can you add your own data to the system?
6. How flexible is the output?
7. How easy is the system to use?
8. Can you "test-drive" the system?
9. How much support is provided by the vendor?
10. How much does it cost?

Source: Several questions are adapted from the list developed by Marci L. Belcher in Martha Farnsworth Riche's article "Computer Mapping Takes Center Stage," *American Demographics,* June 1986, p. 30.

portant questions you should ask when thinking about a computer mapping system.

FIRMOGRAPHICS

The next step, after the geographic bases have been specified and determined, is to analyze a battery of relevant demographic variables. Realize that geographics and firmographics are among the most widely used segmentation variables in industrial markets.

In a study of segmentation variables used by leading companies in South Africa, it was reported that geographics was the most popular base (87 percent). Demographics, usage rate, and buying situation were tied for second place (62 percent). Application/use (also called end use), psychographics, and values were the third most commonly used variables (50 percent). Benefits, purchasing organization, and other variables were infrequently used by these companies.[7]

The U.S. government publishes a wealth of relevant business demographics—e.g., U.S. Business Census Reports (Construction, Manufacturing, Mineral Industries, Retail Trade, Transportation, Wholesale Trade, etc.), business census reports by state, *County Business Patterns,* and so forth. Local, county, and state agencies nicely augment the federal publications.

Also, do not forget the prominent role of the private sector in the mix (*Dun's Census of American Business,* Dun & Bradstreet (D&B) reports, Hoover's, *Manufacturing USA, Markets of the US for Business Planners, Survey of Buying Power,* etc.). D&B's MarketPlace software is a combination database and mailing list service that has been widely praised by many small and medium-sized B2B marketers. MarketPlace uses D&B's database of over 10 million U.S. businesses. More than forty data elements for each business are provided, allowing target marketing by location, size, industry, key personnel, etc.

Business Segmentation Bases

Business demographics or firmographics are similar in concept and purpose to consumer demographics but vary in purpose (see Table 4.1).

TABLE 4.1. Business versus Consumer Demographics

Demographic Category	Business Demographics	Consumer Demographics
Age and stage (of life cycle)	Number of years firm has been in business; stage of product/industry life cycle	Age distribution; family/household life cycle
Financial factors	Sales; profits; market share	Income; occupation; education
Market size	Number of potential customers; number of locations, stores, plants; number of employees	Population; number of households/families; household/family size
Ownership factors	Own or lease establishment (store, office, plant, warehouse); own or lease property and equipment; length of time at facility	Homeowner versus renter; type of dwelling; household mobility/stability
Industry structure/social class	Market/industry position; high-tech versus low-tech; goods, services, information; NAICS/SIC/NACE codes	Lower-lower to upper-upper class; geodemographic/lifestyle clusters (such as PRIZM)

The length of time a firm has been in business and the stage of its industry/product life cycle can be useful segmentation dimensions. New companies do not have established relationships with vendors and can be good targets for computer equipment distributors, accounting and law firms, and a multitude of other products or service providers. Growing companies are in an expansion mode and are ripe for major investments in plant and equipment and marketing/promotional services. Mature companies make sizable purchases but often have well-entrenched relationships with sellers. Firms on the decline will cut back on their spending and buy selectively in categories relevant to their business situation, e.g., image-based public relations, specialized management consultants, etc.

Targeting customers based on sales volume is a common approach used in business markets. Large companies have different needs and purchasing policies than their smaller counterparts. In one study of industrial high-tech companies, a national sample was divided into two groups based on sales volume: small (less than $10 million annual sales) and nonsmall (over $10 million annual sales). Other studies may identify medium-sized firms as $10 million to $300 million in revenues, with large companies exceeding $300 million. Analyses by client profitability or market share can also be insightful in selected situations.

The U.S. Small Business Administration (SBA) publishes size standards based on the number of employees as well as revenues. While these are typically used for loan or government procurement programs, they can also be informative in segmenting business markets. Traditionally, the small/nonsmall breakpoint was 500 employees, although this may vary by industry sector. Some temporary service agencies may choose to target microenterprises having twenty or fewer employees. Similarly, the number of customers or sites that an organization has may be used to segment markets.

Business ownership factors can impact purchase decisions. For example, consider a factory that owns its equipment but is operating at only 60 percent production capacity. Market segmentation opportunities may consider new products, international markets, customization for key clients, and even manufacturing goods for other companies under its brand name.

Industry structure via accepted business sectors or norms (e.g., high-volume versus low-volume machines) and generalized business classification systems have been a mainstay of industrial marketers for years (the latter is our focus—see the next section). Standard Industrial Classication (SIC) codes have recently been replaced by the North American Industrial Classification System (NAICS) in the United States, Canada, and Mexico. Europe's NACE system has also received attention by industrial marketers.

NAICS and NACE

Good-bye, SIC—hello, NAICS! Standard Industrial Classification codes, which served business marketers well for many years, were replaced (the process began in 1997, with changes ongoing) by a more relevant system, the North American Industrial Classification System. SIC codes, in existence for more than sixty years, transitioned from a U.S. government statistical data facilitator to a customer/supplier tool for industrial marketing.

SIC analysis provides a useful first-cut approach to business segmentation. For example, a national uniform supply company regularly buys seven-digit D&B data on computer tape and CD-ROM and targets channel end users by industry type. Approximately 80 percent of its sales are rental uniforms to laundries, 15 percent to end users, and 5 percent direct.

Outwater Plastics, a New Jersey firm selling formed millwork to builders, remodelers, and architects, reaped dramatic gains in new business via SIC analysis. Using eight-digit SIC lists from D&B Marketplace software (iMarket, Waltham, Massachusetts), Outwater doubled their overall direct-mailing response rate to 2.74 percent. In addition, the company found a profitable new niche market that generated a 14 percent response rate. Overall, sales increased by 60 percent.[8]

In its current incarnation, NAICS (rhymes with "snakes") is an evolving, responsive industry categorization tool that is useful for segmentation, forecasting, market share analysis, research, and planning. There are several, notable improvements of NAICS over SIC. There are twice as many major industry group sectors (see Table 4.2 for the list of these twenty categories). There is a much stronger emphasis on the new economy, reflected by the inclusion of many new services and technology sectors. This results in a more detailed directory consisting of 1,170 industries—358 of these are new and 250 of them are services producing.[9] For example, the new Information sector, which was not represented in the SIC manual, is comprised of more than fifty subsectors. The resulting six-digit market identifier, the NAICS code, replaces the basic four-digit SIC code (an example is provided in Table 4.3). Finally, the NAICS system is regional in scope; Canadian and Mexican industry analysis is built into the framework.

The beauty of the NAICS system should be its widespread acceptance (note, SIC analysis was a staple part of industrial marketer's toolkits for many years). Many marketing references, both public (Census Bureau) and private (such as Dun & Bradstreet and Informa-

TABLE 4.2. The NAICS Sectors

Code	Industries
11	AGRICULTURE, FORESTRY, FISHING AND HUNTING
21	MINING
22	UTILITIES
23	CONSTRUCTION
31-33	MANUFACTURING
42	WHOLESALE TRADE
44-45	RETAIL TRADE
48-49	TRANSPORTATION
51	Information
52	FINANCE AND INSURANCE
53	REAL ESTATE and Rental and Leasing
54	Professional, Scientific and Technical Services
55	Management of Companies and Enterprises
56	Administrative and Support, Waste Management and Remediation Services
61	Educational Services
62	Health Care and Social Assistance
71	Arts, Entertainment and Recreation
72	Accommodation and Food Services
81	Other Services (except Public Administration)
92	PUBLIC ADMINISTRATION

Source: U.S. Census Bureau, North American Industry Classification System, 1997.

Note: Sectors in capital letters formed the foundation areas of the 1987 Standard Industrial Classification.

TABLE 4.3. The NAICS Hierarchy

NAICS Level	Industry Description	NAICS Code
Sector	Information	51
Subsector	Broadcasting, telecommunications	513
Industry group	Telecommunications	5133
Industry	Wireless carriers, except satellite	51332
U.S. industry	Paging	513321

Source: <www.census.gov/epcd/www/naics.htm>.

tion Access Corporation), will use the NAICS code as a basic data-gathering unit. Therefore, market analysis through multiple sources is feasible. Anecdotal and scholarly evidence recommend the use of SIC/NAICS codes as tools for segmenting and targeting business markets. Because product complementarity and technological association are clearly significant in many such categories, these codes offer a useful starting point for defining markets.[10] This approach may be especially valuable when there are no strong demand-side factors delineating market boundaries. Furthermore, SIC analysis helps managers avoid the error of drawing market boundaries too narrowly.

The NAICS association provides as a free service a fast keyword search engine with over 19,000 "plain-English" industry codes/descriptions at <http://www.naics.com/search.htm>. NAICS products (manuals, CD-ROMs, etc.) cost from US$35 to $200 and are now available from the following link: <http://store.yahoo.com/naics/ntisnaicman.html>.[11]

The NAICS/SIC system does have some key limitations, however. First, the basic master reference is updated infrequently—about every ten years. Second, product classes do not always correspond with marketers' needs (may be too broad or too narrow). Third, NAICS data do not necessarily correspond to actual geographic market boundaries. They assume all markets are North American and neglect import competition. Fourth, the NAICS reclassification has changed U.S. small business size standards that may be important in government contracting and loan programs. A final limitation is the non-disclosure rule imposed by government publications. This means that information for a sole establishment in a geographic market cannot be released. If that firm was a potential customer of yours, you would not have access to data from public sources about that company.

Although the NAICS/SIC approach is a convenient and informative tool for analyzing markets, research has found that a majority of high-tech and industrial marketers do not use this tool.[12] Hence, education in how to effectively use NAICS is desirable. Also, detailed proprietary coding systems may be useful for business marketers. In its current form, NAICS analysis is probably best used as a secondary variable in conjunction with other industrial segmentation dimensions.

A second major industrial classification system is the European Union's NACE, an acronym for "nomenclature generale des activites dans les Communautes Europeennes," which translates as the European Community Classification of Economic Activities. As Table 4.4 shows, NACE is consistent with ISIC (the United Nation's International Standard Industrial Classification of all Economic Activities). The NACE system is also evolving; for example, the United Kingdom's Standard Industrial Classification of Economic Activities (SIC) is undergoing a major revision dubbed "operation 2007" to be consistent with NACE, ISIC, and its North American equivalent NAICS.[13] This initiative would be advantageous to global marketers for data collection and analysis. Cross-national comparability can help greatly in international segmentation and strategy development.

SUMMARY

As you will see, many dimensions can be utilized for segmenting business markets. The basic options discussed in this chapter include geography, business demographics (firmographics), and NAICS/NACE codes.

Geographic analysis is the logical starting point for industrial market segmentation. This information is low cost and readily available. Regional marketing is on the rise. Often, geographic insights can tell us a great deal about customer purchase patterns. Geographic bases for segmentation include market scope (global, national/regional, or local) and geographic market measures (census classifications, standardized market area measures, and population density and climate-related factors). It is a good idea to use various geographic bases—standardized and custom—to define markets.

The U.S. Census Bureau and private vendors offer good, basic geodemographic products for marketers. Computer mapping has emerged as a valuable support tool for business segmentation for progressive companies. The next three chapters explore important be-

TABLE 4.4. EU Statistical Classification of Economic Activities (NACE revision 1.1, Final Draft 2002)

Description		NACE	ISIC
Agriculture, hunting, and forestry	A	01-01.50	011-0150
Fishing	B	05-05.02	050-0502
Mining and quarrying	C	10-14.50	101-1429
Manufacturing	D	15-37.20	151-3720
food products, beverages, and tobacco	DA	15-16.00	151-1600
textiles/textile products	DB	17-18.30	171-1820
leather/leather products	DC	19-19.30	191-1920
wood/wood products	DD	20-20.52	201-2029
pulp, paper/paper products, publishing and printing	DE	21-22.33	210-2230
coke, refined petroleum products, and nuclear fuel	DF	23-23.30	231-2330
chemicals/chemical products and man-made fibres	DG	24-24.70	241-2430
rubber and plastic products	DH	25-25.24	251-2520
other nonmetallic mineral products	DI	26-26.82	261-2699
basic metals/fabricated metal products	DJ	27-27.85	271-2899
machinery and equipment n.e.c.	DK	29-29.72	291-2930
electrical and optical equipment	DL	30-33.50	300-3330
transport equipment	DM	34-35.50	341-3599
furniture, manufacturing n.e.c.	DN	36-36.63	361-3699
Recycling	DN	37-37.20	371-3720
Electricity, gas, and water supply	E	40-41.00	401-4100
Construction	F	45-45.50	451-4550
Wholesale and retail trade; repair of motor vehicles, motorcycles, and personal and household goods	G	50-52.74	501-5260
Hotels and restaurants	H	55-55.52	551-5520
Transport, storage, and communication	I	60-64.20	601-6420
Financial intermediation	J	65-67.20	651-6720
Real estate, renting, and business activities and consulting	K	70-74.87	701-7499
Public administration and defence, compulsory social security	L	75-75.30	751-7530

Education	M	80-80.42	801-8090
Health and social work	N	85-85.32	851-8532
Other community, social, and personal service activities	O	90-93.05	900-9309
Activities of households	P	95-97.00	950-9700
Extraterritorial organizations and bodies	Q	99-99.00	990-9900

Source: <www.fifoost.org/database/nace/nace-en_2002c.php>.

havioral segmenting approaches such as product usage, benefits (common buying factors), organizational psychographics, purchasing criteria, and adopter categories. The use of multiple business segmentation bases should be considered to provide the richest view of potential market segments and target markets.

Chapter 5

Usage Analysis

Twenty percent of the customers account for 80 percent of the turnover.

Vilfredo Pareto (1911)

Industrial and technology companies typically use account size and industry classification as an initial basis for identifying and targeting markets. While these data are readily accessible, they often provide little insight about how specific goods and services are actually used (and how much are used) by customers. Therefore, usage analyses should be employed as a business segmentation dimension. Consider the marine market as a case in point. A fabric manufacturer may provide basic acrylic fabrics for power and sailboat covers as well as higher-value, custom-designed seat covers for inside the boat.[1]

Usage segmentation can assist in strategic marketing, resource allocation, relationship building/customer retention, and profit planning. Custom Research, Inc. (CRI), a Minneapolis-based, marketing research firm was able to cut its customer base in half yet triple its revenues and double its profits over a ten-year period ending in 1998. This was accomplished by practicing individualized "surprise and delight" marketing for three dozen high-volume/high-margin clients (CRI's core partners), hand-picking and growing profitable new accounts (averaging $200,000 annually), and systematically eliminating more than 100 low-volume/low-margin customers.[2]

If you analyze your individual purchase behavior (e.g., think about grocery shopping), you will notice that there are many products that you buy on a regular basis or in large quantities. Many other items you purchase less frequently, with a vast majority (tens of thousands) of goods seldom if ever bought. This scenario is the basis for product usage segmentation: segments are identified and targeted based on a compilation of product consumption levels within a given market. Usage dimensions also recognize that individuals may act differently depending on their situation or use occasion. For example, a purchasing agent may be a conservative, fact-seeking buyer at the office and at home be an impulsive free-spender.

END USE ANALYSIS

Arguably, a firmographic variable (see Chapter 4), with the end use approach, the final application of the product is the segmenting base. Industrial products can take many forms, including raw materials, work-in-process, and finished goods. The end use of the product has a definite impact on the purchase decision. (Is it a relatively insignificant, perhaps replaceable, part or is it a critical component of a machine?)

A five-step segmentation process can be useful for industrial and high-tech markets.[3] Product type (systems/equipment, components, or materials) is the first consideration. Original equipment manufacturers (OEMs) or aftermarkets (maintenance, repair, and overhaul market, or MRO) provide the second segmentation cut. Steps three and four are SIC/NAICS level and customer applications. Finally, geography, common buying factors, and buyer size complete the segmentation analysis in business markets.

Input-output analysis is closely related to product end use. This technique recognizes that most industrial transactions pass through a channel of users. By analyzing a series of intermediary sales, a company can more accurately focus in on its actual target markets. You now know how much of your product is being used and by whom. Such production/consumption data are available from such sources as *County Business Patterns, Survey of Current Business, Sales and Marketing Management,* Department of Commerce publications, trade associations, and private research firms.

The *Thomas Register of American Manufacturers* is a multivolume directory useful for targeting industrial markets. Although most businesspeople use it as a supply source, you can find new customers through the register, too. Let us assume that you developed an industrial component that was of interest to aircraft or automotive jack producers. The directory identifies several dozen prospects for your product. Customer searches can also be narrowed down by state, area code, or specific words mentioned in company descriptions. The *Thomas Register,* now available on CD-ROM, allows you to receive ads by fax, view textual information, print labels, and telephone prospects—all from the convenience of your friendly PC.[4]

USAGE SEGMENTATION

Segmenting markets by consumption patterns can be most insightful for understanding the customer mix. Sophisticated direct marketers use customer purchase probabilities to assess which and how many catalogs to send to buyers. Hence, differentiated marketing strategies are needed for various user groups: first-time users, repeat customers, heavy users, and former users. By classifying customer accounts based on usage frequency and variety, companies can develop effective and profitable strategies for retaining and upgrading customers. As Box 5.1 shows, there are many highly informative, low-cost applications of usage analysis that should be considered by management.

BOX 5.1. Usage Segment Categorization

- Heavy, medium, light, former, and nonusers (categorized as HU, MU, LU, FU, and NU or A, B, C, D, and X)
- Heavy half segmentation (80/20 rule)
- Users versus nonusers
- Competitive users
- Loyal (degree) versus nonloyal customers
- Product/service applications by user group
- Adopter categories—innovators, followers, laggards; lead users
- Geographic comparisons—customer penetration indices, growth rates

---

For example, a "businesspersons'" hotel may grade clients based on the number of rooms booked annually. The key accounts are A1 users; these are large organizations that reserve more than 500 room nights and conference facilities. A2 customers also book 500-plus rooms without the conference arrangements. A third category of heavy users is the A3 account; this is a solid, loyal customer that generates 100 to 500 rooms annually. Descending usage levels of B customers are considered medium users. Finally, C accounts represent light users. A C4 guest may visit the hotel only once a year.

By classifying customers into usage categories, management can readily design appropriate strategies for each market segment. The objective is to move customers up the usage ladder, where possible, e.g., turn a C1 into a B5 or an A3 into an A2 customer. The implication of usage analysis is that all buyers are not equal; some (the heavy users) are clearly more valuable than others.

Medium users (B customers) form the solid foundation of a business. Revenue enhancement strategies such as cross-selling or value-added services can be used to keep these customers satisfied and grow their business. Regular telephone calls, e-mails, and personal sales calls are suggested to stay in touch with this group. By knowing who the better customers are (the As and Bs)—through geographics, firmographics, benefit studies, or behavioral research—a profile of "typical users" is established. This information is very helpful in planning subsequent customer attraction/conquest marketing efforts. Realize that the marketing information system, your database, plays a pivotal role in customer analysis and decision making (this is discussed near the end of the chapter).

For unprofitable customers (generally the C accounts), companies must find new, low-cost ways to serve them effectively. Computer technology such as Web sites or Web catalogs can be useful in this regard. Occasional contact (perhaps quarterly) via direct mail, e-mail, e-newsletters, reminder postcards, and phone calls maintains adequate communication with low-volume users. In some cases, it is advisable to sever the relationship with unprofitable customers.

A good understanding of purchasing patterns helps firms keep customers and gain a larger share of their business. Share of customer (an important customer retention measure) has supplanted market share (a customer attraction objective) as the relevant performance dimension in many business markets. For example, if a company is able to increase a customer's share of business from 20 to 30 percent, this can have a dramatic impact on market share and profitability.

RFM (recency, frequency, and monetary value) analysis is a helpful tool in evaluating customer usage and loyalty patterns. Recency refers to the last service encounter or transaction; frequency assesses how often these customer contact/company experiences occur; and monetary value probes the amount that is spent, invested, or committed by customers for the firm's products and services. A few years ago, this author purchased about $75 worth of brochure materials from a direct-marketing firm for a one-time consulting project. This eager vendor immediately placed our writer into the preferred customer category and began sending him expensive catalogs about every three weeks without any follow-up orders.

RFM analysis tells us that this is not sound marketing practice since this company essentially treats all one-time "tryers" as *best* customers. Note that this transaction fared poorly on all of the critical RFM dimensions—recency (three-plus years ago), frequency (a single purchase), and monetary value (relatively low).

A more effective strategy is to classify customers via usage analysis (as previously described) and design differentiated marketing approaches for each target market. According to Rust, Zeithaml, and Lemon, FedEx categorized its customers internally as the good, the bad, and the ugly based on profitability. These marketing scholars propose a generalized, four-tier usage segmentation system (see Box 5.2).[5]

In sum, usage analysis can greatly assist in customer retention activities. Think about how to "hold" heavy users and key accounts, upgrade light and medium users, build customer loyalty, understand buying motives to meet/exceed expectations, use appropriate selling strategies for each targeted usage group, win back "lost" customers, and learn why nonusers are not responding to a value proposition.

Note, customer relationship management (CRM), an expensive information technology, is also frequently used by large companies for

---

BOX 5.2. Customer Tiers

1. *Platinum Tier*—the company's most profitable customers, typically heavy users, not overly price sensitive, willing to invest in and try new offerings, and are committed customers of the firm
2. *Gold Tier*—profitability levels not as high as Platinums, seek price discounts, less loyal, and use multiple vendors
3. *Iron Tier*—essential customers who provide the volume needed to utilize the firm's capacity, but whose spending levels, loyalty, and profitability are not substantial enough for special treatment
4. *Lead Tier*—customers who cost the company money, demanding more attention than they are due given their spending and profitability, sometimes problem customers who complain about the firm and tie up resources

Source: Adapted with the permission of The Free Press, a Division of Simon & Schuster Adult Publishing Group, from *Driving Customer Equity: How Customer Lifetime Value Is Reshaping Corporate Strategy* by Roland T. Rust, Valarie A. Zeithaml, and Katherine N. Lemon. Copyright © 2000 Roland T. Rust, Valarie A. Zeithaml, Katherine N. Lemon. All rights reserved.

---

business usage analyses. Unfortunately, this much-hyped alternative has been criticized recently for promises unfulfilled, i.e., not being an effective and profitable communications system with customers. As a result, the CRM business has experienced declining sales, ongoing consolidation, and unhappy end users.[6] (An in-depth discussion of CRM is beyond the scope of this book.)

CONCEPTUALIZING AND OPERATIONALIZING USAGE DIMENSIONS

Usage analysis consists of two components: usage frequency (how often the product is used) and usage variety (the different applications for which a product is used).[7] For example, two account executives may both use their laptop computers three hours daily (same usage frequency). One salesperson may only do e-mail and call reports, while the other prepares client proposals, analyzes financial spreadsheets, manages projects, as well as e-mail and call reports (greater usage variety).

To analyze markets based on usage patterns, it is first necessary to classify users into specific consumption categories. An often-used method is heavy users versus medium users versus light users versus nonusers for a particular good or service. For example, you probably are familiar with the 80/20 rule, or Pareto Principle. This business axiom states that approximately 80 percent of your sales come from only 20 percent of your customers (also, note that generally about 80 percent of sales come from 20 percent of the goods or services offered). Hence, knowing who your best customers are and which products are your fast sellers offers you a tremendous marketing edge.

Strategy Consulting, Inc.'s usage analysis revealed that 26 percent of its business (long-term clients) accounted for 84 percent of its profits. In addition, 22 percent of its revenues (mergers and acquisitions) yielded 87 percent of its profits. Operational projects (33 percent of its revenues) were found to be a losing proposition for the company, and, subsequently, future inquiries in this area were farmed out to specialist consultancies.[8] Two additional, detailed examples of the effective use of ABCD analysis by Novartis Generics and the 80/20 principle by Fast Industries are presented in Business Segmentation Insight 5.

It is essential to defend your core business base since heavy users (A accounts) are primary attraction targets to key competitors. These highly profitable customers require frequent advertising, promotions, and sales calls, and ongoing communication efforts.

In business and professional service markets, your very best customers should be earmarked as key accounts based on customer ranking (e.g., the 100 most important customers), minimum sales volume level (e.g., $1 million in annual revenues), or market share (e.g., an annual account exceeds 1 percent of the total business). Four helpful guidelines for key account management (KAM) are offered by McDonald and Rogers.[9] These are summarized in Box 5.3.

BOX 5.3. Guidelines for Key Account Management (KAM) Programs

1. Partnership KAM should be the goal. Three- to five-year contracts and up to forty performance criteria can be established. Partnership KAMs improve processes, increase quality, and reduce costs.

2. Individualized client strategic marketing plans are seldom done but most successful. Areas to develop include, but are not limited to, achievements, customer value, cost savings, problems, and opportunities.

3. Compensation plans that work best for KAM positions are 51 to 80 percent salary plus bonuses tied to specific criteria that take a long-term view.

4. Other relevant planning/implementation issues:

   - Do a SWOT (strengths, weaknesses, opportunities, threats) analysis for each key account.

   - Assess the degree of entrenchment with the client (potential for switching).

   - Design a relationship management program.

   - Think long-term contracts.

   - Consider growth prospects.

   - Find similar "others."

   - Measure time commitment with the client.

   - Understand sales and nonsales functions (advice, installation, service, support, etc.).

   - Give key accounts special treatment/status.

   - Communicate regularly with client.

   - Provide value-added initiatives.

Source: Adapted from Malcolm McDonald and Beth Rogers, *Key Account Management* (Oxford, England: Butterworth-Heinemann, 1998).

BUSINESS SEGMENTATION INSIGHT 5:
USAGE SEGMENTATION APPLICATIONS

Example 1: Novartis Generics

The Novartis Corporation, a European company, is one of the world's largest pharmaceuticals company.[10] Novartis Generics, a key division in the company, like many pharmaceutical firms is a strong believer in usage analysis. The 80/20 rule is a well-accepted maxim in the pharmaceutical industry. For example, it is known that about 20 percent of the doctors write about 80 percent of prescriptions overall, and within selected product categories.

Using a 2 × 2 segmentation grid, Novartis Generics classifies doctors based on customer attractiveness and relative competitive position. While the latter dimension is self-explanatory, the former consists of the number of prescriptions written, whether they prescribe generics, interest in the product line, and company loyalty. Based on their potential, doctors are placed into one of four groups. The ABCD analysis is as follows: A—top clients, B—high potentials, C—low potentials, and D—unsatisfactory.

As Table 5.1 shows, A and B segments are the focus of a new product launch. The C segment is a secondary target and D customers are not actively pursued. The resulting ABC approach is further adapted based on country-specific strategies used in various worldwide regions. Among the marketing implications of usage analysis for Novartis Generics include segment profitability assessments; long-term market potential of prescriptions by region, doctor, and specialty; internal corporate positioning within segments; competitive analysis; strategic differentiation; sales force allocation and promotional resource deployment; and the need to provide exceptional service to heavy users.

Example 2: Fast Industries Key Account Strategy

Fast Industries is a plastics manufacturing company located in Fort Lauderdale, Florida.[11] The company is the world's largest producer of label holders and serves leading retail store chains, including Wal-Mart, Target, CVS Drugs, and Michael's Crafts.

TABLE 5.1. Novartis Generics' ABC Analysis

Segment/ Name	Strategic Focus	Annual Number of Visits per Doctor	Service Level	Promotional Emphasis
A/Top clients	Customer service	Medium	High	Sampling—low level
B/High potentials	Marketing/ promotion	High	Medium	Sampling, mailings, promotions—high levels
C/Low potentials	Serve physicians cost-effectively	Low	Low	Sampling—low; mailing and promotions—medium levels

Fast Industries is undergoing a transformation from a smaller family-run, mom-and-pop manufacturing company to a more professionally structured, staffed, and managed organization. Because of the recognition that customer retention is more important than customer attraction, much effort was spent ensuring that Fast's most valuable customers perceived this change as positive and were more likely to remain a customer. Two major strategic initiatives that played a central role in the new marketing strategy were the 80/20 principle and the value proposition.

The 80/20 principle was integral in determining the focus and location of Fast's most important customers. Although there are over 2,000 retail chains in the United States, due to variations in the number of stores and size of stores per chain, it was estimated that about ninety of them will purchase 90 percent of the store fixtures components that Fast can offer. Currently, Fast does business with thirty of these retailers, and for each of these key accounts, delivering superior customer value is a top management priority.

Next, the value proposition was utilized to determine the exact nature of each customer's relationship with Fast. Since there are four basic providers of value to a customer (price, service, quality, and image), all customers were surveyed by their respective sales representative on exactly why they do business with Fast and what aspects of value were derived from doing business with the company. Using an internally designed strategic assessment form based on the value proposition, it was found that no relationships with Fast were based on image or price alone, but that service and quality were laden with further nuances. Service to one customer might mean high levels of in-stock orders. To another it might mean ease in placing an order. To yet another it may be constant attention from a sales representative. Quality as a criterion can be broken down into components as varied as the product's engineering and design, on-time delivery, and/or the product being packed and billed correctly.

A second assessment tool was a SWOT (strengths, weaknesses, opportunities, threats) analysis conducted at individualized and aggregate levels, and information was gathered from each strategic customer. An assessment of Fast's overall relationship with all accounts plus a future forecast and recommended strategy were developed. What was perhaps most unique about this analysis was that it sought to describe the strategic position of business relationships in terms of the value proposition.

Through the sound application of strategic marketing principles rooted in segmentation and customer value, Fast Industries is now designing and delivering superior products/services to its most important customers—and it is working in a big way. This customer retention strategy had a significant impact on profitability for the year 2001, with revenues increasing by 20 percent and profits increasing by 25 percent.

ASSESSMENT OF THE USAGE DIMENSION

Although usage analysis has at times been treated as a step-child as a segmentation base, this "sleeper" is still a very viable technique that can provide you with great insight in most business markets. Segmenting markets based on usage categories provides four major benefits:

1. It is a useful dimension for understanding markets; e.g., computer users purchase diskettes, zip drives, laser paper, print cartridges, service contracts, etc.
2. It can increase consumption among heavy users in moderately competitive markets. One study identified five different approaches by which heavy user indices could be calculated.[12] These solutions impact the allocation of marketing resources and efforts.
3. It can increase consumption among light and medium users in highly competitive markets; a case in point is the hotel chain example discussed earlier in the chapter.

4. By providing new benefits, it is possible to attract nonusers or neglected segments. Systematic segment tracking and evaluation provides direction for reaching overlooked market opportunities.

Marketers need to be cognizant of three shortcomings associated with the usage dimension. First, usage segments are often difficult to explain through traditional demographics only. In many markets, additional segmentation bases should be employed, e.g., benefits, organizational psychographics, and/or purchasing criteria exposure. Second, there are some inherent problems associated with targeting the heavy user segment. Other companies are likely also to recognize the value of the heavy user. Therefore, competition for customers in this segment can be great. All heavy users are not purchasers for the same reasons. Customers may want price, performance, service, or quality. Since customers have different needs, further subsegmentation within the heavy-user category is usually advisable. Also, heavy users are not product loyal; they tend to buy heavily within a product category but often have little allegiance to individual products, services, or companies. Industrial buyers tend to be more loyal than consumers, however. Third, there are some definitional problems in usage analysis. For instance, how do we distinguish between a heavy, medium, and light user? Also, what criteria should be used in specifying consumption segments? These and other questions must be answered by the market segmentation analyst.

In general terms, usage segmentation does not have the widespread acceptance of demographics, nor the explanatory value of benefit segmentation or organizational psychographics (it is descriptive not causal information). Additional research is needed to maximize the value of usage analysis in the marketplace. This can be accomplished by treating usage measures as both primary segmentation bases (a dependent variable) or as a complementary tool (an independent variable) that can extend other segmentation findings.

Usage analysis has much to offer since it is a flexible, low-cost, and easy-to-use marketing research technique. Goods and services can be analyzed for consumption levels on both a unit or dollar volume basis.

Marketing implications regarding usage segmentation relate to brand/company loyalty, promotion, and marketing information. Loyalty can be built through ongoing customer programs (e.g., frequent flyers) and offering long-term service contracts and relationship marketing practices. Advertising and selling efforts should be customized to meet the needs of various customer groups. Customer invoices, credit records, industry directories, trade papers, and databases can be tapped to garner valuable data about past buyer behavior and how it can be used to predict future customer purchases.

Many firms have a small core of key accounts accounting for a substantial proportion of their sales. In industrial markets, heavy users require regular sales calls and perhaps a dose of LGD (lunch, golf, and dinner) marketing. Infrequent customers can be informed of your company's activities and new products through quarterly newsletters, occasional telephone calls, and e-mail communications. Also, realize that winning back former users is generally easier than creating new customers. Segmentation Skillbuilder 5 lists ten key usage questions that should be addressed by marketers (you may want to add others).

SEGMENTATION SKILLBUILDER 5:
USAGE ANALYSIS—KEY ISSUES

1. Who are the users?
2. Who are the nonusers?
3. How do heavy users differ from light users? (Think about the number of orders, unit sales, and dollar sales.)
4. Have you identified A, B, and C customers?
5. Can you win back former customers?
6. How do your customers differ from your competitors?
7. How loyal are your customers?
8. What are the applications of product usage by user group?
9. What are the geographic differences by market? (Compare customer penetration rates and growth patterns of various regional markets; develop usage indices.)
10. Are you using a marketing information system effectively?

A marketing information system (MKIS) captures the vital information needed for analyzing product usage groups. In addition to recording key demographic and psychological characteristics, one business consultant tracks clients' key advisers (attorneys, bankers, and CPAs), publications they read, organizational affiliations, and the trade shows and seminars they attend.[13] This information separates prospects from suspects. A strong MKIS must be able to produce segmentation data at various levels of aggregation—a requirement that is easily met with today's powerful information technologies.[14] A complete MKIS consists of the following four subsystems:

1. A marketing records system tracks recurring sales and customer data. (Remember, your customer is your most important marketing asset!)
2. A marketing intelligence system monitors market conditions (e.g., competition, syndicated data, sales rep input, etc.).
3. A marketing research system obtains and inputs primary data about your customers (review Chapter 3 guidelines).
4. A marketing tools support system consists of corporate intranets, databases, graphics programs, statistical packages, and other computer software. This permits the user to access and analyze customer data from subsystems 1 through 3. Hewlett-Packard does this extremely well. This allows them to find the segments of greatest marketing opportunity for their business units and new products.

SUMMARY

From a segmentation perspective, a differentiated approach to target marketing based on usage segments and key account management are two important initiatives to implement. Should your company focus its resources and energies on heavy, medium, light, or nonusers?

Marketers must realize that all customers are not the same. Clearly some users are much more important than others—the A customers or heavy users. This target market requires special attention via increased investment, dedicated sales/support personnel, time commitments, etc. Key account management should be reserved for the top tier of the A customer class. Individualized marketing plans should be prepared for these clients, a relationship manager/team assigned, and one-to-one marketing implemented.

B customers (the "bread-and-butter") or medium users often provide the core base for corporate accounts. Strategies for keeping and growing these customers must be designed. C customers or light users should be served in cost-efficient programs such as telephone call centers or Web sites.

Usage segmentation and relationship management are the key marketing activities to obtain the desired results of retaining more customers, getting better customers, upgrading customer relationships, and using existing customers as advocates for acquiring new customers.

Chapter 6

Benefit Segmentation

There is nothing to suggest that benefits have lost their role as one of the best possible starting points for segment definition.

Russell I. Haley (1999)

Is it price/value, quality, reputation, service, or, perhaps, some combination of other factors (e.g., buyer-seller relationships, customization, delivery reliability, durability, ease of use, innovation, warranties, etc.) that drives your customers' purchase decisions? Business marketers can turn to benefit segmentation to help answer this critical question. In addition, an analysis of benefits is also very useful for identifying gaps in the market between customer expectations and experiences, competing on technology, product line management and new product development, positioning via communication research and strategies, distribution decisions, and pricing policies.

For example, Bayer Diagnostics "point-of-care" (or POC) market consists of all in vitro diagnostic testing (e.g., blood gas, critical care, urine chemistry, etc.) performed outside of a central lab by health care professionals who may not be trained laboratory technicians. While this division had a good handle on geographics (site locations), firmographics (customer type), and usage (volume), a major segmentation initiative was needed to assess behavioral factors, as shown in Figure 6.1. (*Note:* the questions of where, who, and how much were discussed in Chapters 4 and 5.) The "why" question can be answered through benefit segmentation (reviewed in this chapter), while the "how" and "other variables" queries can be explored via purchasing approaches (see Chapter 7). Technology, innovation, cost, loyalty, at-

FIGURE 6.1. A Proposed Segmentation Approach for the POC Market

titudes, and international variables such as economic development indicators, market growth rates, segment size, and culture were identified as potential "others."

At the time of the segmentation training, the POC diagnostics testing market was growing approximately 7 percent annually. Bayer's objective was twofold: to defend existing accounts and to generate double-digit growth to outpace the market (a protect-and-grow strategy). This future-focused approach assessed opportunities systematically and required a strategic rationale for allocating resources and targeting customers. According to Rick Kates, Bayer Diagnostics Marketing Manager, POC Testing Segment, the "new" segmentation model should be comprehensive, differentiated, and validated and lead to sustainable competitive advantage.[1]

CONCEPTS AND APPLICATIONS OF BENEFIT SEGMENTATION

The marketing concept is based on the satisfaction of customer needs. Benefit segmentation follows this guiding philosophy by asking a related marketing-oriented question: What is this product going to do for me, the customer? Benefits are the sum of product advantages or satisfactions that meet a customer's needs or wants. They extend beyond product features and serve to satisfy physical, emotional, or psychological needs. Two clear examples of what a benefit is are often cited in personal sales training: "Sell the sizzle, not the steak" and "People don't buy drill bits, they buy round holes."

CompuRent leases computer equipment to banks, hospitals, schools, nonprofit organizations, and industry. Advantages of renting/leasing versus purchasing include these: customers can try before they buy, customers may have a short-term need for the equipment, cash flow is controlled, and expenditures can be applied toward the purchase. Entrepreneurs are also appealing to other benefit segment niches, such as those seeking preowned computer equipment.

Benefit segmentation probes deeply into users' buying motives. A compilation of key benefits is analyzed in determining pertinent market segments. A primary benefit or a summation of benefits is often featured and used for segment identification purposes, for example, the *value seekers*.

In an Irish Sea study of shippers purchasing freight transport services between Great Britian and Ireland, three benefit segments were found. The *route-sensitive* shippers (35 percent of the market) were primarily interested in the convenience of the route, while the *price-sensitive* ones (40 percent) were seeking a low-cost service, and the *not-price-sensitive* users (25 percent) were expecting a high level of service care.[2]

Generally, a product will have one primary usage. However, through effective research, other potentially profitable benefit segments may be revealed. In many cases, the composition of benefit segments can differ markedly from geodemographic classifications alone. A study of nonintelligent data terminals indicated that traditional business segmentation bases such as company size and SIC codes do not act as surrogate measures for benefits sought.[3]

Using survey data, an industrial supplier selection study of Indian purchasing managers assessed fifty-one decision choice criteria. The research found that organization ownership and, to a lesser extent, annual sales volume could qualify as surrogate measures of benefit segments. In contrast, industry type, respondent characteristics (position, age, education, experience), and size of purchase were not found to be adequate bases for segmentation; hence, they were not surrogates for benefits.[4]

Values and past purchase behavior can have a great impact on benefits sought by buyers. According to the confirmation-disconfirmation paradigm, a positive experience means that the customer will seek repeat satisfaction; a negative experience leads to avoidance. Many companies are now cultivating the long-term, benefit-seeking customer.

As an example, an Australian study of users of electrical and mechanical maintenance services used common buying factors to identify four market segments: *relationship-seeking, price-sensitive, high-expectation,* and *customer-focused service users.* Significant differences among the segments were found based on five clustering variables (price, organization size, core service needs, customer focus, and relationship between user and provider); problem areas (the gap between expectations and performance); and industry concentration.[5]

Different customer segments are attracted to various product and service offerings based on the package of benefits offered to them. By segmenting an industrial market through analyzing common buying factors (benefits sought), marketing strategies can be tailored to the needs of specific customer sectors. Hence, customer action (interest, inquiries, and orders) and postsale satisfaction are more likely to result through this approach than through unfocused marketing initiatives.

An electrical components producer segmented its market based on common buying characteristics. One segment consisted of high-volume buyers that were extremely price sensitive. Another segment of small-lot buyers insisted on high quality and special features but were not noticeably price conscious. The manufacturer was able to meet the low-price requirements of the former segment by raising prices in the latter 25 percent, with no appreciable loss of business.[6]

One of the hottest areas in marketing in the past few years has been customer value, which is closely related to benefits sought by customers. Business Segmentation Insight 6 explores this linkage.

BUSINESS SEGMENTATION INSIGHT 6:
CUSTOMER VALUE AND BENEFITS

The concept of customer value (CV) is as old as ancient trade practices. In early barter transactions, buyers carefully evaluated sellers' offerings; they agreed to do business only if the benefits (products obtained) relative to the cost (traded items) were perceived as a fair (or better) value. CV may be best defined from the customer's perspective as a trade-off between the benefits received versus the price paid. Value is created when product and user come together within a particular use situation. Thus, each transaction is evaluated as to a dissatisfaction, satisfaction, or high-satisfaction experience from a value perspective. These service encounters impact customer decisions regarding the benefits delivered (not just promised) and whether to form long-term relationships with organizations.

Value-based thinking originated at General Electric after World War II. CV-driven marketing strategies help organizations in ten areas:

1. Understanding customer choices
2. Identifying customer segments
3. Increasing their competitive options (for example, offering more products)
4. Avoiding price wars
5. Improving service quality
6. Strengthening communications
7. Focusing on what is meaningful to customers
8. Building customer loyalty
9. Improving brand success
10. Developing strong customer relationships[7]

Service, Quality, Image, and Price: The Essence of Customer Value

Providing outstanding customer value has become a mandate for management. In choice-filled arenas, the balance of power has shifted from companies to benefit- and value-seeking customers. CV can be expressed in many ways.

The SQIP approach states that value creation is a combination of service, product **q**uality, **i**mage, and **p**rice. Top-notch companies often differentiate themselves and create legendary reputations largely due to singular attributes. While a focus on a key attribute is advisable, firms must meet acceptable threshold levels with respect to each dimension; formidable global competition provides little room for weakness in any area.

The service factor must reign supreme in value-creating organizations. FedEx built its reputation based on a strong value proposition that guarantees package delivery by 10:30 a.m. the next morning—"When it absolutely, positively has to get there."

A recent study by CustomerRespect.com found that only 41 percent of Fortune 100 companies responded to an Internet communication within two days, 22 percent eventually responded, and amazingly 37 percent never responded! (The insurance sector was the most responsive; drug companies were the least responsive.) Hence, this research indicates that nearly six out of ten giant companies fail to take their Web presence seriously.[8] Furthermore, realize that customers defect for service reasons more than two-thirds of the time.

Hewlett-Packard is obsessed with product quality and innovation. Broderbund Software also knows that quality products are essential to its business success. It has used innovative offerings and niche marketing to compete effectively in the educational and gaming software markets.

Value innovation can be fostered in companies by reducing investment in business units that are *settlers* (offer me-too products and services), increasing investment in *migrators* (businesses with value improvements), and using corporate entrepreneurship initiatives to create *pioneers* (businesses that represent value innovations). Research on the source of high growth in diverse organizations found that only 14 percent of new business initiatives were true value innovations; yet these breakthrough concepts yielded 38 percent of total revenues and an impressive 61 percent of total profits.[9]

e-Bay's cultlike following highly values this e-tailer's image and philosophy as well as its incredible merchandise selection at good prices. e-Bay's business model has recently attracted a stream of corporate sellers such as Dell and IBM to market to buyers via this site.

In contrast to FedEx, the U.S. Post Office's priority mail service suffers because of a weaker value statement. While the flat-rate, one-pound envelope is a nice deal at $3.85, its relatively slow two- or three-day delivery is a serious drawback. Many customers often send items priority mail because of image rather than speed—the red, white, and blue package looks more important than regular mail when it arrives on a client's desk. A 30 percent price increase (to $5.00) to ensure two-day delivery would greatly strengthen this product, though it would still be about a third of the price of competitive offerings.

Others, such as some advertising specialties companies and discount seminar companies such as CareerTrack, are committed to offering great prices. Realize that low cost is only part of the value equation—value is the total purchasing experience. This may include such customer benefits as product-service mix, the latest/greatest technology, six sigma quality, corporate reputation, respect for customers, time savings, postsale service, etc.

Since trade-offs exist among the SQIP elements, companies cannot expect to be market leaders in all areas. The cost of developing and sustaining a four-dimensional leadership position would be overwhelming. Clearly, we can see that customer value is a much richer concept than just a fair price; superb service, top quality, and a unique image are also highly valued by target markets. Realize that CV is a multidimensional construct. Using insights gained from segmentation research, companies can vary their emphases on SQIP to explicate their value proposition while providing the benefit packages desired by target markets.

PROS AND CONS OF BENEFIT SEGMENTATION

The prudent use of benefit analysis provides marketers with a new perspective and added insight into market situations. When properly executed, this approach is one of the most powerful means to identify and exploit markets. Here are two examples.

Case one: Four solution-based, high-tech segments were found in researching the mobile professional market via a value-added analysis. These are individuals who conduct business out of their office at least 20 percent of their time using cell phones, computers, pagers, and other technologies. The *specialized solution* customer is the "be-first" buyer requiring specialized hardware and one-of-a-kind software. The *customized solution* user wants to solve business problems not technical problems. *Value solutions* are aimed at midlevel managers rather than senior technologists. Finally, *packaged solutions* (which are known solutions to known problems) are geared to the mass market and sold via retail channels.[10]

Case two: Forty-eight customer service attributes were analyzed in a high-tech application in emerging industries. Two segments emerged. For Segment A, customer service was important in vendor selection (this segment was comprised of companies that are small but have larger purchase requirements than Segment B). In contrast, customer service was not an important issue for Segment B. The two potential target markets responded differently to product, promotional, and price factors as well.[11]

The Benefits of Benefit Segmentation

The three major advantages of benefit segmentation are as follows:

1. *Widespread application:* Benefit segmentation is an appropriate segmentation base for researching domestic and international business opportunities. It can be effective for assessing market segments and niches for goods, services, and ideas.
2. *Flexibility:* Benefit segmentation is a method with great adaptability. Here are three examples:
   - Benefit segments can be derived through a variety of approaches, including, but not limited to, focus groups, the Delphi technique (a group of expert opinions), in-depth interviewing, and quantitative research (mail surveys, telephone and personal interviews). Analytical methods for forming benefit segments can span the gamut from tabulation of opinion to multivariate analysis (cluster, conjoint, factor, discriminant, regression analyses, etc.).
   - Common or custom segment classifications can be used in the study. In past segmentation studies, some generic benefit segment groups have been called *conservatives, inner-directed, rational man,* and a host of other explanatory segment names.[12] A customized typology maximizes the value of the research findings by offering sophisticated segmenters a better way for identifying and selecting target markets.

- Benefit segmentation can be used in collaboration with several other closely related segmentation bases. These include buyer adopter categories, firmographics, industrial psychographics, product usage, etc.
3. *Causal basis:* The strongest argument in favor of benefit segmentation, however, is that it is based on cause-and-effect factors rather than descriptive factors. Russell Haley, who pioneered the benefit segmentation methodology, advocates a three-step approach consisting of exploratory research, scale development work, and quantitative measurement.[13] Because benefit segments recognize why customers buy—their purposes and product desires—a direct relationship exists between motivations and purchasing patterns. In Segmentation Skillbuilder 6, Haley offers you some basic tools that you will need to begin applying benefit analysis to your market situation.[14]

The Limitations of Benefit Segmentation

In many respects the shortcomings of benefit segmentation resemble those of psychographic research, namely, complex data collection and analysis (large number of data inputs, probabilistic sampling, multivariate statistical analyses) and cost factors (on the higher end of the pricing scale for segmentation studies). An additional limitation of concern to marketers is human behavior. Although individuals may say they want specific, rational benefits from products, they sometimes do not act as they indicate and deviate from their stated purchasing intentions.

THREE BRIEF EXAMPLES
OF BENEFIT SEGMENTATION
IN BUSINESS MARKETS

Dr. Gary Mullet is a well-respected marketing researcher and statistician who has conducted hundreds of segmentation studies for a variety of clients over the years. He explains that factor analysis and other multivariate techniques (cluster and discriminant analyses) are valuable tools in the "Swiss Army knife" methodology of benefit segmen-

SEGMENTATION SKILLBUILDER 6:
USING SEGMENTATION GRIDS TO IDENTIFY BENEFIT SEGMENTS
FOR YOUR COMPANY

This exercise presents a six-step process to identify customer market segments for your firm. Although the focus of this approach centers on benefit segmentation, other physical and behavioral dimensions are incorporated into the planning and research framework to provide a detailed segment profile.

Methodology

1. List several major benefits that customers are likely to seek in choosing your firm's goods or services (record these benefits in Table A).
2. Show this list to a prospective customer and ask the respondent if there are any additional benefits important to him or her in selecting your firm's products. Add these new benefits to Table A and record all of them in Table B.
3. Ask this respondent to rate the benefits numerically in Table B using the following importance scale:

Most important benefit	= 4
Second most important benefit	= 3
Third most important benefit	= 2
Fourth most important benefit	= 1
All other benefits	= 0

4. Collect similar marketing data from a sample of other respondents using the same procedure. Add in new benefits and continue recording these data in Table B.
5. After all data have been collected, note respondents with similar response patterns (numerical highs and lows). These respondents are members of specific market segments.
6. List key benefits by segment on the segmentation grid (Table C). Using your keen judgment, complete the segment description given the attributes provided. (*Note:* Typically marketing research findings assist us in this process.) When the segment column is completed, provide a name representative of the overall market characteristics for the segment. Continue with this approach for the other market segments.

Table A: Major Benefits

1. _____
2. _____
3. _____
4. _____
5. _____
(more?) _____

Table B: Respondent Benefit Grid

Benefit	Customer					
	1	2	3	4	5	(more?)
1.						
2.						
3.						
4.						
5.						
(more?)						

Table C: Segmentation Grid for Your Company

Attribute	Segment				
	1	2	3	4	5
Motivations/benefits					
Usage situations					
Usage by product type					
Frequency of usage					
Degree of loyalty					
Image of your firm					
Media preferences					
Adopter categories					
Key demographics					
Geographics					
Other descriptors					
SEGMENT NAME					
SEGMENT SIZE					
STRATEGIC IMPLICATIONS					

Source (and Recommended Reading): Adapted from Russell I. Haley, *Developing Effective Communications Strategy: A Benefit Segmentation Approach* (New York: John Wiley and Sons, Inc., 1985).

tation analysis. In a study contracted by a computer manufacturer, he shares relevant data and insights on this powerful approach.[15]

Professional computer users were asked to evaluate the importance of computer attributes and sales outlet/manufacturer attributes in their purchase decision. Using benefit segmentation methodology, an initial set of thirty-six variables was reduced to twelve, resulting in the identification of four benefit segments (see Box 6.1 and Table 6.1).

Terri Albert recently investigated the steel manufacturing supply chain for a customized, concrete reinforcement product. A summary of the relevant buying criteria and key user groups are listed in the two-factor, benefit segmentation solution shown in Table 6.2.[16]

Finally, the packaging division of the Signode Corporation used in-house documents (sales records) and sales force judgments on price and cost-to-serve to determine customer segments in the mature steel strappings market. Using cluster and discriminant analyses, four buying behavior segments were identified. *Programmed buyers* used rules of thumb to allocate purchases to a few vendors. *Relationship buyers* are knowledgeable about the competition and tend to pay higher prices for relatively less service; they are interested in forming longer-term "partnerships" with Signode. *Transaction buyers* want price over service and are a switching threat if competitors meet their product needs at reduced costs. *Bargain hunters* are high-volume accounts seeking major price discounts and maximum service; they are likely to defect if there is any incident of dissatisfaction.[17]

SUMMARY

Once a basic descriptive understanding of a market exists (typically via geodemographics and usage analysis), business marketers should turn to behavioral dimensions to gain greater insights on why and how customers buy and the specific attributes that they value. Behavioral segmentation studies are designed to assess customer benefits/benefit packages (our focus in Chapter 6) and/or evaluate organizational psychographics and purchasing criteria (review Chapter 7).

BOX 6.1. Benefit Statements for the Computer Industry Study

On a scale of 1 = not at all important to 10 = extremely important, respondents were asked to rate the importance of each of the following in their decision to acquire a new computer.

1. Is one of the most reliable available
2. Is on the leading edge of technology
3. Has one of the highest resolution screens available
4. Is able to store a large number of files and data
5. Is one of the lightest available
6. Allows the user to print high-quality output, including words and graphics
7. Uses the same size diskettes as other personal computers or technical workstations that the user needs to interact with
8. Connects easily to a local area network
9. Has good workmanship
10. Is easy to expand with additional hard disk storage capacity
11. Does not take up much space
12. Allows several computing tasks to be performed simultaneously
13. Has one of the very lowest prices available
14. Is sold by people who are well informed about computer technology
15. Is easy for a nontechnical person to get up and running in a few hours the first time
16. Is portable
17. Is sold by people who will always help with user problems
18. Uses icons and a mouse to operate the software
19. Can operate on a battery
20. Has software that is very easy to learn
21. Is sold by people who provide software and hardware together in a tailored solution package
22. Allows the user to easily combine graphics, words, and numbers on a page
23. Runs the same operating system as other computers that the user needs to interact with
24. Is sold by people who will provide training
25. Is one of the fastest available

(continued)

(continued)

26. Communicates easily with larger computers
27. Allows the user to do very complex graphics
28. Is sold by people who will fix it in a few hours if it breaks
29. Is made by a company your management approves of
30. Uses software that operates the same way as software the user is familiar with
31. Is able to run a very large selection of software
32. Will not become obsolete quickly
33. Is easy to expand with additional purchasing power
34. Runs only custom-designed software that performs a very specific task or function
35. Is acquired from a location that sells at the lowest prices but provides little assistance
36. Runs software designed specifically for your industry

Source: Gary M. Mullet, "Benefit Segmentation in Practice," *Journal of Segmentation in Marketing,* 3(1), 1999, pp. 13-36. Reprinted with permission of The Haworth Press, Inc.

TABLE 6.1. Mean Summary for the Benefit Segmentation Variables in the Computer Industry Study

Variables	Segments			
	Independent	Nonnetwork	Specialized	MAC/Windows
Dealer	5.66	6.77 a	6.85 a	6.71 a
MAC/Windows	5.31 a	5.40 a	5.46 a	**6.29**
Expandable	6.36	6.77 a	6.84 a	7.04 a
Reliable	7.46	7.83 a	7.85 a	8.09 a
Portable	3.87 a	4.46 b	4.11 ab	4.18 ab
Specialized	4.08	5.89	**7.46**	3.27
Easy	5.68	6.92 a	6.16	6.65 a
Compatible	7.58 a	7.31 a	7.61 a	8.15
Network	5.99	**3.41**	7.57 a	7.50 a
Low price	6.07 a	5.88	6.06 a	5.72 a
Not obsolete	7.74 a	8.29 b	6.35	8.14 ab
Management OK	**3.21**	8.29 a	8.71	8.36 a

Source: Gary M. Mullet, "Benefit Segmentation in Practice," *Journal of Segmentation in Marketing,* 3(1), 1999, pp. 13-36. Reprinted with permission of The Haworth Press, Inc.

Note: Letters indicate means *not* significantly different. Boldface numbers represent key scores for salient variables.

TABLE 6.2. Benefits Sought and the Steel Manufacturing Supply Chain

Buying Criteria	Component 1: Technical Advice and Support	Component 2: Account Servicing (Relationship Building)	Key Supply Chain Group
Technical publications, information	X		Structural engineer
Answering technical questions	X		None
Design suggestions or templates	X		Precaster
Engineers on staff to discuss options	X		Supplier
Economics of different materials for construction	X		Structural engineer
Using comparison tables of the two materials	X		DoT representative
Notification of materials during construction job		X	DoT representative
Sales incentives to try other materials		X	Supplier
Service after the sale is completed		X	Fabricator
Relationship-based pricing		X	Contractor

Source: Adapted from Terri C. Albert, "Need-Based Segmentation and Customized Communication Strategies in a Complex-Commodity Industry: A Supply Chain Study," *Industrial Marketing Management,* 32, 2003, pp. 281-290.

Benefit segmentation groups customers by similarities in buying motives. In this chapter, we examined various facets of benefit segmentation. These include results of past research studies, corporate examples of benefit segmentation and derived segments, advantages and disadvantages of this base, methodological issues, and practical guidelines. Such material can be most helpful to market segmentation managers as foundation material for preparing organizations to undertake the next step—consider using this valuable research-based segmentation approach. While the time and investment in benefit segmentation can be substantial, the potential paybacks of this causal methodology are workable, flexible marketing strategies that can greatly enhance your bottom line.

Chapter 7

Purchasing Behavior and Organizational Psychographics

A good customer should not change his shop, nor a good shop change its customers.

Chinese proverb

This chapter continues our discussion of behavioral segmentation; you recall we examined benefit segmentation in Chapter 6. The opening section presents a brief review of how purchasing factors differ in industrial markets. Next, we will explore three key approaches to B2B segmentation. These include Bonoma and Shapiro's nested approach (an integrative, industrial segmentation model), business psychographics, and buyer adopter categories.

HOW BUSINESS MARKETS ARE DIFFERENT

Prior to designing the industrial segmentation research plan, it is important to recognize four major differences between consumer and B2B markets: (1) scope of the geographic trade area, (2) product/market factors, (3) nature of the purchase decision, and (4) closeness of the customer.

Scope of the Geographic Trade Area

The area an industrial marketer serves is typically larger than the one served by neighborhood retailers or personal/professional service firms. Granted, major retailers such as Target and Pizza Hut and service organizations such as H&R Block and Kinko's are found nationally, but they appeal to localized customer groups. It is common for the industrial firm to conduct business regionally, internationally, and globally, as well as via the Internet.

Despite this larger trade area focus, the customer base for the industrial firm is generally highly concentrated. For example, a supplier and distributor of industrial pumps and motors serviced accounts throughout the southeastern United States, but the majority of its sales came from its own backyard (North Florida). As another example, Silicon Valley (California), Route 128 (Boston), and the Research Triangle (North Carolina) are all areas of intensive high-tech activity. While it may appear that industrial market areas are easier to quantify and target than consumer markets, purchasing decisions are usually more complex.

Product/Market Factors

Most industrial sales are larger than those in consumer markets. Of course, there are consumer purchases of automobiles, boats, or houses, but, for individuals, these are rare purchases. Generally, consumer sales are relatively small compared to industrial sales of equipment, materials, components, products, or services (periodic reorders of industrial parts and supplies may be small orders, however).

As a corollary to this, there are generally fewer potential customers for the company to target in industrial markets. For example, Boeing is faced with only a limited number of prospective buyers for its aircraft. At times, this smaller customer pool can play havoc with the best-laid marketing plans. Dependency on a small core of customers often leads to large variations in revenues and profits (greater peaks and valleys), as the firm acquires or loses major accounts or macro-environmental conditions change due to economic turmoil or prosperity, political uncertainties, global terrorism concerns, etc.

Industrial sales come from derived demand (not final demand), which makes the firm more susceptible to cyclical market pressures. As an example, steel producers historically have been greatly dependent on automobile sales.

Nature of the Purchase Decision

A complex consumer decision is a joint one between a husband and wife to buy new bedroom furniture. In industrial markets complex decision making occurs on a regular basis. Often, many people will be involved in purchase decisions. Special justifications, authorizations, and approvals will be needed, and months can pass before a sale is transacted. The industrial salesperson is confronted with more intelligent, calculating, and rational buyers than are typically found in the consumer sector. On the positive side, once a customer has been "sold," loyal, lasting customers are often the result.

Traditionally, the North American bus fleet was segmented based on geographic area and size of the bus fleet. A new approach based on purchasing factors resulted in six decision process segments (e.g., the low bid and manufacturer reputation segment) and six product feature segments (e.g., the drive train and not drivers segment).[1] Thinking outside of the box (i.e., not using traditional industry segmentation) can provide companies with a unique marketing edge in the marketplace.

Closeness of the Customer

In their highly acclaimed book *In Search of Excellence*, Peters and Waterman stressed the importance of getting close to customers and listening to their needs and wants.[2] Industrial companies are naturally closer to their customers, although buyer satisfaction levels may vary from poor to excellent depending on how well they implement the marketing concept—an organization-wide effort to satisfy customers at a profit.

Closeness in industrial markets is nurtured because personal selling is the most effective promotional strategy, the sales force typically goes on-site to the buyers' premises, and long-term customer relationships often develop. In addition, it is easier to stay in touch with your market through trade journals that comprehensively cover industry news and views, trade directories that provide detailed marketing information about firms, and trade associations that share knowledge about markets. Furthermore, new technological tools such as databases, direct and group e-mails, online chats, and mobile tele-communications help keep sellers and buyers connected. However, action—creating and delivering responsive, customer-centric marketing programs—is needed to truly meet the needs of B2B buyers.

The buyer-seller relationship impacts customer loyalty and the likelihood for switching vendors. "Soft targets" are potential customers who have weak relationships with their current vendors; often this is due to features or supplier performance gaps. A soft target segmentation strategy identifies customers with similar needs who may be responsive to customized sales and service strategies.[3] How entrenched are your customer relationships?

THE NESTED APPROACH

In a comprehensive review of the industrial segmentation literature, Dick Plank noted that there were three approaches for selecting segmentation bases: (1) unordered segmentation notions (a single segmentation dimension is chosen with no specific rationale for how it was selected), (2) two-step notions (such as the macro/micro-segmentation reviewed in Chapter 4), or (3) a multistep approach. He adds that there has been limited work on this latter segmentation tool with the exception of the Bonoma and Shapiro's nested model that is discussed next.[4]

The nested approach is a practical and comprehensive means for segmenting business markets. It consists of the following five nests (bases) and related segmentation variables:

1. *Demographics*—industry, company size, and customer location
2. *Operating variables*—technology, user status, and customer capabilities
3. *Purchasing approaches*—purchasing function organization, power structures, buyer-seller relationships, and purchase policies/criteria
4. *Situational factors*—urgency of order fulfillment, product application, and size of order
5. *Buyers' personal characteristics*—buyer-seller similarity, attitudes toward risk, and buyer motivation/perceptions[5]

Generally, marketers should work systematically from the outer nests (numbers 1 through 3) to the inner ones (numbers 4 and 5) because data are more available and definitions clearer. However, the inner nests (situational and personal variables) are often more useful. In situations where knowledge and analysis exist, marketers may begin at a middle nest and work inward (occasionally outward). A balance between the simplicity and low cost of the outer nests and the richness and expense of the inner ones is desirable to maximize the value of the segmentation analysis.[6] An overview of the nested approach is depicted in Figure 7.1. In addition to the visual presentation of the model, questions relevant to the industrial segmentation variables are presented in Table 7.1.

An insightful adaptation of the nested framework was recently applied to reseller markets (retailers and wholesalers).[7] Manufacturers can use three sets of segmentation bases—external, internal, and interpersonal—to segment markets and find appropriate target markets. Specific variables include type of intermediary, size, location, life cy-

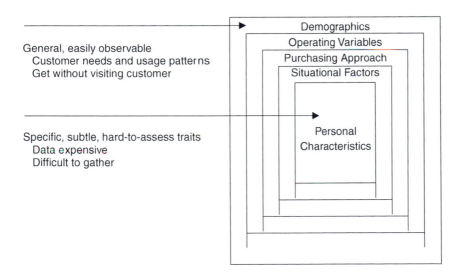

FIGURE 7.1. Industrial Market Segmentation—A Nested Approach (*Source:* Reprinted with permission from Thomas V. Bonoma and Benson P. Shapiro, *Segmenting the Industrial Market* [Lexington, MA: Lexington Books, 1983].)

TABLE 7.1. The Nested Approach—Key Questions

Characteristic	Segment by	Questions
Demographics	Industry	Which industry to focus on?
	Company size	Can you produce enough for large needs?
	Customer location	What geographical areas?
Operating variables	Technology	What customer technologies?
	User status	Heavy, medium, light, nonusers?
	Customer capabilities	Need many or few services?
Purchasing approaches	Purchasing function	Centralized, decentralized?
	Power structures	National account versus field engineer-dominated, finance, etc.?
	Nature of relationships	Strong relationships or most desirable companies?
	Purchasing policies	Leasing, service, price, bid?
	Purchasing criteria	Quality, service, price?
Situational factors	Urgency of filling order	Quick delivery?
	Specific application	Certain or all applications?
	Size of order	Large or small orders?
Buyers' personal characteristics	Buyer-seller similarity	Values similar to ours?
	Attitudes toward risk	Risk-taking, risk-avoiding?
	Loyalty	High loyalty to suppliers?

Source: Reprinted with permission from Thomas V. Bonoma and Benson P. Shapiro, *Segmenting the Industrial Market* (Lexington, MA: Lexington Books, 1983).

cle position, form of ownership, and financial condition (external variables); markets served, current product purchases, infrastructural factors, location of purchasing, and reseller's perceived image (internal variables); and benefits sought, reseller's use of product, buyer-seller similarities, purchasing policies, and characteristics of individual buyers (interpersonal).

Although the nested approach was developed in the mid-1980s, it holds up remarkably well to the segmentation challenges of industrial markets, and, in fact, no new multistep models have earned widespread attention by business marketers. Ben Shapiro's thoughts on the nested approach twenty years after its development are presented in Business Segmentation Insight 7.

BUSINESS SEGMENTATION INSIGHT 7:
IN CONVERSATION WITH DR. BENSON P. SHAPIRO

"The 'Nested Approach' is still applicable to industrial markets today in the twenty-first century. It is still relevant but changes are taking place. Although still useful, what is happening is it is much harder to segment markets than in the seventies. It is much more important to segment markets when possible . . . more is being done in this area since everyone is doing demographics. This is commonplace in market research today. It is also easier to get information on demographics versus in the seventies. What will give today's marketers a competitive edge is those who can unlock the key to address personal characteristics of the buyer and situational factors that can be tapped into by the seller. The three outer rings are still there but should play far less a role in the importance than the two innermost rings. They now play the most important role in nested segmentation in the twenty-first century. It must be noted that segmentation is much harder to do today than ever before. Potential research into other factors that could affect industrial segmentation should be considered."

Source: Telephone interview conducted by Dr. Steven V. Cates on September 19, 2002. Reprinted with permission.

While custom models generally work best in an organization, the nested approach is one of the best ways for energizing a company to think about initiating a strong segmentation-based marketing strategy. I have found that half-day or day-long strategic planning sessions with key decision makers using the nested approach can yield tremendous insights on segmenting business and high-tech markets. Segmentation Skillbuilder 7 provides a realistic scenario for applying this simple, yet valuable approach to a better understanding of your market situation.

SEGMENTATION SKILLBUILDER 7:
USING THE NESTED APPROACH TO SEGMENT
YOUR MARKET

Your boss, the Director of Marketing, has just returned your market-ing plan draft for 200_, with this comment in large red ink: "Let's look for a new approach to segmenting our market!" Recently, one of your product managers attended a seminar on B2B segmentation and sug-gested that your company consider using the "nested approach" to seg-ment its market. The three of you meet, review notes on how this seg-mentation process works, and contemplate how to adapt this approach to your business/industry.

Use the nested approach to identify appropriate segmentation bases and variables for segmenting your market (review Figure 7.1, Table 7.1, and Business Segmentation Insight 7 as refresher material).

Suggested Reading: Thomas V. Bonoma and Benson P. Shapiro, *Seg-menting the Industrial Market* (Lexington, MA: Lexington Books, 1983).

BUSINESS PSYCHOGRAPHICS

When you travel are you a *happy camper, worry wart,* or *grumpy guest?* An exploratory, national study found that 41 percent of business-persons enjoyed traveling, an equal percentage worried about airline and hotel safety, and 18 percent had few good things to say about business trips.[8]

The term *psychographics* was coined by Emanuel Demby, a mar-keting researcher, nearly forty years ago. Demby's definition (edited) of psychographics is "the use of psychological, sociological, and an-thropological factors, self-concept, and lifestyle to determine how the market is segmented by the propensity of groups within the market—and their reasons—to make a particular decision about a product, per-son, or ideology."[9] In addition to personality traits and lifestyles (also known as AIOs, for activities, interests, and opinions), attitudes, be-liefs, motivations, opinions, trends, and values have been used in psychographic studies to obtain meaningful marketing information.

A longtime powerful consumer segmentation technique, psychographics has recently been discovered by innovative business marketers. Since individuals ultimately make all buying decisions, psychographics can be an important dimension in understanding purchase behavior and influences. This higher-level analysis assumes that the industrial marketer already has a good perspective on the market situation and wants to expand the analysis to include characteristics of the target firm's decision maker(s). Now, let us consider several practical examples.

Personality research found that individuals could be classified by five geometric shapes:

1. Boxes are neat, organized, and highly structured (accountants, computer programmers).
2. Triangles are self-assured, respected, and leaders (executives, entrepreneurs, politicians).
3. Rectangles are going through life changes and are unpredictable (college graduates, new employees).
4. Circles are concerned about good interpersonal relations and peace (nurses, secretaries).
5. Squiggles are creative, idea people who are not detail oriented (artists, scientists).[10]

An industrial psychographics study, at the wholesale level, was useful for matching salespeople with purchasing agents based on personality traits and business-related factors. The four market segments identified were the *social buyers, factual buyers, social sellers,* and *factual sellers.* A partial list (ten of fifty-two) of the psychographic items used in this research instrument, measured on a 1 (disagree) to 6 (agree) scale, is shown in Box 7.1.[11]

A Fortune 50 pharmaceutical company used a belief-based, segmentation study of physicians. Based on this analysis, the firm eliminated 39 percent of the doctors on its call panel (two market segments) due to their lack of belief alignment with the brand's proposition. The remaining, highly targeted physicians (61 percent of the market, comprising three segments) increased the brand's total prescriptions by 50 percent within a year, while the nondetailed physicians cut their

---

BOX 7.1. Selected Business Psychographic Statements

- I prefer window seats when traveling, say, by plane.
- Material things are very important to me.
- Before having an appliance repaired, I'll try to fix it myself.
- When I attend a business meeting, I frequently offer new ideas.
- On weekends and vacations I try not to think about the office.
- I seek out the opinion of others before making decisions.
- I am detail oriented.
- I like to work long hours.
- I prefer to make my own investment decisions.
- Many salespeople visit their buyers too frequently.

Source: Adapted from Seymour H. Fine, "Buyer and Seller Psychographics in Industrial Purchase Decisions," *Journal of Business and Industrial Marketing,* Winter-Spring 1991, pp. 49-58.

---

prescription writing by only 10 percent during that period. Overall, this resulted in a $15 million increase in annual incremental sales and a $7 million reduction in sales/marketing expenses that is projected to yield $68 million in a three-year net present value (NPV) gain for the brand.[12]

Corporate culture was found to be a useful psychographic dimension for segmenting the market for corporate financial services in an entrenched marketplace. Using cluster analysis, three market segments were revealed: *happy doers* (36 percent of the sample), *middle-of-the-roaders* (34 percent), and *satisfaction seekers* (30 percent). *Happy doers* tended to be highly satisfied with top-of-the-line suppliers and vendor decisions were generally made by a top executive. This group was more operations oriented than customer focused. Multiple buying influences were present, the use of several suppliers was evaluated in purchase decisions, and personalized service was critical to the *middle-of-the-roaders.* While multiple buying influences were also important with *satisfaction seekers,* this segment also was characterized by customers/prospects who were unhappy with their vendor's pricing and performance.[13]

Pros and Cons of Organizational Psychographics

Psychographic research is being used more frequently in business market segmentation studies for four major reasons: target market identification, understanding buyer behavior, strategic marketing, and minimizing risk.

Customer differences extend beyond demographics to unobservable characteristics (for example, corporate strategy). Strategic types *(defenders, prospectors, analyzers,* and *reactors)* and strategic orientation *(customer orientation, financial orientation, internal orientation, human relations orientation,* and *research and development orientation)* were found to be useful organizational psychographics in a study of car phone purchases by Dutch firms (a new-buy purchase decision). In contrast, the two firmographic variables, firm size and industry, had little explanatory value with respect to the adoption or nonadoption of the proposed technology.[14]

Business market analysis means understanding people, relationships, and psychological drivers. By analyzing purchase motives, marketers can better understand why buyers act the way they do in the marketplace. As an example, small and medium-sized family business clients of professional service providers (accounting, insurance, and law firms) were researched using organizational psychographics. Market segments were identified based on CEO motivations for operating the business. In descending order, the eight psychographic segments of family business owners, which ranged from more than a third of the sample to less than 5 percent, were as follows: *loving parents, autocrats, empire builders, fortune hunters, recruits, rebels, status seekers,* and *social benefactors.* These grouping motivations impacted purchasing attitudes and behavior.[15]

Strategic information gathered through a psychographic analysis can permeate all marketing areas of the company. Some examples include product modification and positioning/repositioning, recognizing the importance of price factors, promotional strategies and campaigns, and exploring new distribution methods or improving existing channel strategies.

The cost of a new product introduction, line extension, service offering, or proposed venture can be substantial. Furthermore, almost half of all projects fail (based on five-year profitability). According to research sponsored by the Product Development & Management Association (PDMA), the new product success rate for B2B organizations was 54.5 percent.[16]

By incorporating business psychographics into your firm's product testing and R&D program, project successes are more likely. Often the key ingredient is locating the subtle product or concept variations that customers desire.

Although using psychographic research in business segmentation studies can be very beneficial, there are also two key shortcomings of which the marketer must be aware. These are data collection/analysis and cost factors. Unlike demographics, psychographics is primary research, and a more complex approach to obtaining the marketing information sought by management. Data collection can be problematic due to the large number of questions asked via the survey instrument. Compounding this is the analysis of a voluminous amount of data, requiring the use of multivariate statistical techniques in seeking key marketing relationships.

A well-designed psychographic study is on the upper rung of the pricing ladder compared to other types of segmentation research. It is not unusual to expect to invest $100,000 and up for a complete research package. If cost is a prime consideration for your company, this type of analysis is not an appropriate use of marketing funds. Now that you are reasonably informed about psychographics, you may be ready to initiate a research project in your company. Seventeen points to consider in negotiating for this type of behavioral research are listed in Box 7.2.

VALS and Syndicated Psychographics Services

Although most of the "packaged" psychographic research offerings were designed to better understand consumer markets, some of these services can be readily adapted to business situations since people ultimately make all purchase decisions.

BOX 7.2. A Checklist for Contracting for Psychographic Research

1. Is custom or syndicated lifestyle research required?
2. Is there in-house capacity to assist in the project?
3. Specifically, what are your research objectives (see Chapter 3)?
4. Have you spoken with at least two research firms or consultants with expertise in psychographics?
5. Do they have experience in your market or a closely related market?
6. What are the professional (experience) and academic qualifications (knowledge) of the researcher(s)?
7. Did you review detailed proposals from these research providers?
8. From a methodological perspective, exactly what is entailed in the study?
9. Will the psychographic research be used to identify new market segments, describe existing segments, or predict differences in customer behavior?
10. Can the psychographic research be validated against other syndicated services or your own primary research?
11. What supporting dimensions (in addition to the psychographics) will be used in the study?
12. Will this psychographic segmentation approach respond to changes in the marketplace?
13. How closely will the researcher work with your company in project design, implementation, and strategy development?
14. Is this a one-shot effort, or is an ongoing relationship with the research firm desired?
15. How will the quality of the information be measured?
16. What value do you expect from this study?
17. How much is this answer worth to you?

SRI International's VALS program is a U.S. lifestyle segmentation system (a Japan-VALS is also available) that categorizes customers based on high or low levels of innovation and resources.[17] Three powerful motivators are ideals, achievement, and self-expression. Ideals-oriented individuals are driven by knowledge and principles. Achievement-oriented people seek a clear social position and positive evaluations and rewards. Self-expression individuals are action oriented and make choices that relate to personal challenge. The eight-segment VALS typology is shown in Figure 7.2.

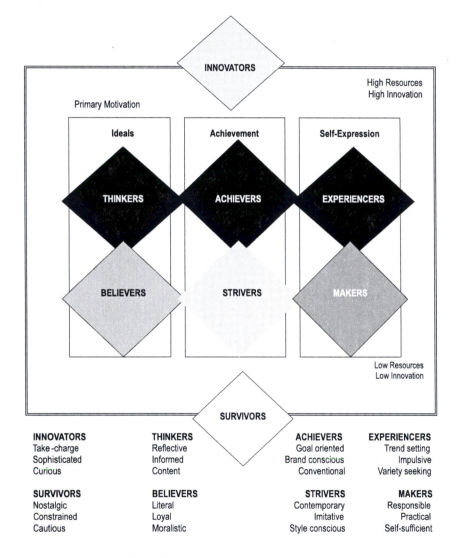

FIGURE 7.2. The VALS Framework and Segments (*Source:* SRI International, Menlo Park, California, <http://www.sric-bi.com/VALS/types.shtml>. Reprinted with permission.)

VALS information has been used successfully to develop new products, create product positioning strategies, target new markets, design advertising campaigns, measure media audiences, and predict business trends. In addition, SRI has joint venture agreements with leading geodemographic clustering firms, such as Claritas and Donnelley, and with product usage/media information providers, such as Simmons. Hence, powerful linked customer analyses are possible.

Other syndicated lifestyle services include the Yankelovich Monitor, the University of Michigan's List of Values (LOV), and products by leading advertising agencies and market research firms. (Check with the American Association of Advertising Agencies and the American Marketing Association.)

BUYER ADOPTER CATEGORIES

Markets can be segmented based on the rate of customer acceptance for new product concepts. According to Forrester Research, today's vendors should consider "technographics" to determine why certain technology products succeed and others fail. Of the twelve technology-based market segments that they uncovered, here are five miniprofiles:

1. *Cyber-snobs* upgrade frequently and invest heavily in trendy technologies.
2. *Fast-forwards* are well-to-do and short of time; they seek time-saving and productivity-oriented technologies.
3. *Handshakers* are successful executives and professionals who let their secretaries do their computing; they believe personal relationships are the key to success.
4. *Mouse potatoes* are affluent, technology-loving individuals who constantly seek new experiences; they are PC-focused and into CD-ROMs.
5. *Traditionalists* are indifferent or hostile to computer technologies; they only adopt proven, ubiquitous products.[18]

Adopter category segmentation is based on two key ideas: the diffusion of innovations and the identification and effective marketing to early users. According to the diffusion literature, there are five categories of new product acceptance: innovators, early adopters, early majority, late majority, and laggards.[19]

Lead users or superinnovators face strong market needs months or years before the bulk of the marketplace and expect to benefit significantly by helping to find a solution to those needs.[20] Innovators may be techies (users excited by the new technology) or visionaries (managers who can see a product's potential for improving processes, enhancing operations, or delivering value to gain a competitive advantage).[21]

From a practical standpoint, we can often say that markets are comprised of three broad adopter categories: "early buyers and tryers," "maybe-laters," and "forget-about-'ems." While adopter category segmentation is useful in many industrial market situations, it is particularly insightful in high-tech markets. The following example illustrates this process based on a segmentation research project conducted by this author (and a colleague) in the cardiac pacemaker market.

Segmentation Example—The Pacemaker Market

The market for cardiac pacemakers has stabilized in the past decade due to pricing pressures caused by diagnosis-related groups (DRGs) and institutional buyers, intense competition, investigations into the need for the products, and regulatory problems. In the short term, manufacturers can improve their market position at the expense of competitors. New product development is a major priority. An automatic pacemaker (pacer) is an implantable device that does not require preprogramming and has sensor inputs that maintain the safest level of patient care.

Semistructured depth interviews with physicians provided adequate data for an exploratory segmentation analysis of the automatic pacer submarket (segment identification was the research objective). Based on the qualitative research, six potential market segments for automatic pacers emerged. Three of these customer segments—the *progressives, black-box devotees,* and *show-me's*—were likely adopters (worth targeting for future marketing activity). Two segments—the *nonbelievers* and *no perceived need*—may eventually adopt the product, although they were not good choices to target for short- to intermediate-term marketing activity. One segment—the *techies*—were likely never to adopt the automatic pacer.

Although many factors were considered in segment formation, one major attitudinal variable (user orientation) was most useful in understanding the automatic pacer market. This was expressed as a primary interest in technology, simplicity, or conservatism in decision making. A brief description of the characteristics of the targeted physician-customer segments is shown in Table 7.2.

TABLE 7.2. Adopter Categories for Automatic Pacers

	Segments		
Variables	**Progressives**	**Black-Box Devotees**	**Show-Me's**
Adopter category	Innovators	Early adopters	Followers
Segment profile	View pacer as technological advancement; will try unproven products	"Nontinkerers"; want simple and reliable products	Like concept; need support/case studies (a large segment)
User orientation	Technology	Simplicity	Conservative
Type of physician	Implanting cardiologists	Implanting cardiologists	Surgeons, referring cardiologists, internal medicine practitioners, electrophysiologists
Hospital type	Teaching	Nonteaching	Nonteaching
Usage rate	High	Average-high	Average
Sources of information	Professional journals, sales reps/materials, colleagues	Sales reps, colleagues	Primarily colleagues
Need for manual overrides	Yes	Uncertain; further research required	Yes

SUMMARY

As marketers have realized that geodemographics and usage are seldom adequate to understand today's complex markets, purchasing factors and organizational psychographics have been employed to segment business markets in recent years.

Business markets differ from consumer markets in four respects: (1) the scope of the geographic trade areas (larger, but more concentrated), (2) product/market factors (larger sales, fewer customers), (3) the nature of the purchase decision (more complex), and (4) the closeness of the customer (more personal contact). These differences must be carefully considered when segmenting industrial and technology-based markets.

The nested approach is a comprehensive segmentation model designed for industrial markets. The five key segmentation bases for analysis are demographics, operating variables, purchasing approaches, situational factors, and buyers' personal characteristics. Buyer adopter categories are particularly insightful in high-tech markets.

The use of multiple business segmentation bases should be considered to provide the richest view of potential market segments and target markets. Next, we will discuss how to turn segmentation research results into successful customer-driven marketing strategies.

PART III:
IMPLEMENTING SEGMENTATION
STRATEGY

Chapter 8

Strategic Target Marketing

If you can't describe your strategy in twenty minutes, simply and in plain language, you haven't got a plan . . . every strategy ultimately boils down to a few simple building blocks.

Larry Bossidy (2002)
Chairman, Honeywell International

Market segmentation can be informative, insightful, innovative, and even interesting, but its real value lies in its ability to be implications oriented—create profitable business opportunities from similar market situations.

Segmentation analysis and strategy planning can be likened to playing cards in several respects. All players (companies competing in a given market) must abide by the same rules (industry regulation) and are dealt cards from the same deck (overall market conditions). Individual players must decide how they will play their hands (strategy) given their resources (finances, skills, strengths, weaknesses, etc.). Some players are financially strong and can outspend their competitors, while others are aggressive and win on their business savvy (i.e., knowing when to hold 'em and when to fold 'em). Market segmentation recognizes that all hands (marketing opportunities) should not be played equally, but rather the players/companies should concentrate on those efforts which provide them the best chance for success. Success results from the best prospects for your goods or services—your target markets.

Building on Darwinian theory, parallels between biological competition and business competition have been drawn. Just as no two species can coexist if they make their living in the identical way, firms that offer the same products, in the same territory, under the same conditions, and with the same clientele cannot coexist equally. Eventually, one will dominate.[1] In this chapter, we will examine the execution of segmentation, i.e., translating research findings into action and tailoring the marketing mix to segment needs and desires.

TARGET MARKET STRATEGY FORMULATION

Market segment mapping is useful for finding growth opportunities, yet relatively few industrial companies use this strategic planning tool effectively. According to Bossidy and Charan, less than 5 percent of the plans they have seen contained useful segmentation information.[2] Most voluminous marketing plans devote a majority of their pages to review product features and promotional material but offer limited discussion of a customer profile, benefits sought, and what is valued in business relationships.

Ideally, segmentation findings can be readily turned into action-oriented, strategic programs, but this is not always the case; strategy formation is not an immediate process. Although most segmentation analyses are data based, strategy development almost requires a sixth sense. There are intangible factors, such as experience and creative insight, that play a role in strategic design. Given the limitations of one chapter, this book presents only a general framework for strategy formulation (specific strategies and tactics must be adapted to your market situation and chosen segments).

Recognize that marketing elements differ in importance in various segmentation studies. For one firm, product factors may be the primary consideration, while in another promotion or distribution can be the central controllable. Secondary issues should not be neglected either, since their impact may also be crucial to developing new marketing programs.

THE THREE BASIC STEPS
TO STRATEGY FORMULATION

A three-step process can be used to develop your target market strategy (see Box 8.1). This process consists of the following components: (1) segment identification, (2) target market selection, and (3) positioning.

BOX 8.1. Segmentation Strategy—
The Three-Step Approach

Step 1: Identify Market Segments

List the submarkets from your segmentation study.

Market Segment A (name):
Market Segment B (name):
Market Segment C (name):
Market Segment D (name):
Market Segment X (name):

Step 2: Target Market Segments

Select key segment or segments for marketing activity.

Primary market (name):
Primary market profile and needs:

Secondary market (name):
Secondary market profile and needs:

Tertiary market (name):
Tertiary market profile and needs:

(continued)

(continued)

Step 3: Position the Segments

Formulate unique marketing strategies.

Primary market (name):
Competitive advantages:
Positioning strategy:

Secondary market (name):
Competitive advantages:
Positioning strategy:

Tertiary market (name):
Competitive advantages:
Positioning strategy:

Segment Identification

The first seven chapters of the book developed a framework for planning and conducting a market segmentation analysis. The end product of such a study is the determination of a given number of homogeneous market segments based on selected segmentation variables and criteria. Now the market has structure, and marketing decisions change from analytical to strategic in nature.

Target Market Selection

Examine the airline industry as a case in point. Customers fly different airlines for a variety of reasons. These include economy, service and amenities, flying to the "right" destination, the airline's reputation, and catering to the business traveler. Which benefit segments should management pursue?

Business marketers must select from the alternative market segments one or more groups to target for marketing activity. Each of the individual segments must be evaluated on its own merits and in conjunction with the capabilities and environmental situation surrounding the firm. This evaluation recognizes that the options are unique and have varying degrees of attractiveness to your firm.

Although several submarkets may seem to be worthwhile for targeting, companies must analyze and balance a multiplicity of tangible and intangible factors in their market selection decisions. This includes customer needs, corporate objectives, the internal environment (in particular, financial and other resources), the external environment, and an overall assessment of opportunities versus problems.

Measuring segment potential helps business marketers in determining which segment(s) to pursue. As Table 8.1 shows, criteria for choosing targets can be qualitative or quantitative. While MBA-trained managers tend to prefer the latter to base decisions on, numbers can be misleading. While multipage spreadsheets "look good," frequently the sales forecasts or profit projections are based on incomplete data, questionable assumptions, or flawed research methodologies. As Business Segmentation Insight 8 explains, companies must carefully assess and weigh key discriminating criteria to find the "best" market segments.

Qualitative criteria can provide powerful guidance with respect to market selection. The nature of business preferred is a good starting point. For example, do the segment opportunities allow the firm to

TABLE 8.1. Criteria for Choosing Target Markets

Qualitative Criteria	Quantitative Criteria
Nature of business preferred	Sales by dollars/euros/yen, etc., sales growth rates
Strategic synergy	Market share
Strengths and weaknesses	Profit potential
Market trends	Customer lifetime value (LTV), customer retention indicators
Geographic coverage	Return on investment (ROI)
Industry structure	Breakeven analysis (BEA), net present value (NPV), payback periods

compete on quality and high margin or exploit the company's sales skills?

General Electric's transformation into the twenty-first century was based on Jack Welch's vision of a boundaryless company that would dominate global markets (be number one or number two in its industry sector), in high-tech, industrial, service, and information businesses. Clearly, lightbulbs and refrigerators were no longer part of GE's big-picture marketing strategy. Other firms may be attracted to particular target markets based on strategic synergy, such as the ability to use existing distribution channels, build on process strengths, or capitalize on excess factory capacity.

BUSINESS SEGMENTATION INSIGHT 8: GUIDELINES ON MARKET SEGMENT ATTRACTIVENESS

Based on research of the United Kingdom's Times Top 1000 companies, Simkin and Dibb found that the three most important criteria for selecting target markets were *profitability, market growth,* and *market size.* Likely customer satisfaction, sales volume, likelihood of sustainable competitive advantage, ease of access of business, opportunities in the industry, product differentiation, and competitive rivalry rounded out the top-ten criteria. (*Note:* Twenty-three items were tested.) The authors conclude that businesses in the United Kingdom should replace their short-term, financially oriented focus with a more long-term, analytical and objective view of market segmentation.[3]

McDonald and Dunbar add that segment attractiveness factors be weighted based on the particular requirements of an organization, for example, growth rate (40 percent), profit potential (40 percent), and segment size (20 percent). They also provide a list of twenty-seven possible, generalized segment attractiveness factors in five major areas: market factors, competition, financial and economic factors, technology, and sociopolitical factors. While the big three—growth, profits, and segment size—offer a reasonable starting point in most markets, they advise that two or three additional metrics be incorporated into the market selection analysis.[4]

Positioning

It is next important to formulate a unique marketing strategy to appeal to the customers you are trying to reach. Although a "me-too" or copycat strategy sometimes works, in the majority of cases, a fresh approach to marketing is required to stand out from the crowd and be successful. The basic premise behind positioning is that the firm must have a competitive advantage to survive or thrive in the marketplace. These advantages can be real (e.g., a better product or lower price) or perceived (e.g., a product that is built to last or backed by a company's reputation).

Positioning is sound marketing decision making based on the facts—the segmentation study findings—plus business creativity. This creative process might call for searching out unique marketing advantages, seeking new market segments that competitors are not cultivating, or developing new approaches to "old" problems. The goal of the positioning strategy is to carve out a market niche for the firm. Perceptual mapping, which has long been used as a modeling technique in consumer markets, has gained favor as a diagnostic tool in industrial settings.[5]

Positioning is increasingly critical to high-technology marketers. A three-level positioning model is shown in Figure 8.1. The core product (Level I) is the device that the company produces. At this short-term positioning stage, differentiating features such as quality, specifications, and price are at the forefront. These variables can be quickly emulated by competitors; hence, there is a need for intermediate positioning. The extended product (Level II) develops the marketing infrastructure and strategic relationships. The total product (Level III) is a long-term positioning strategy. It sells who the company is and what it stands for. Merck's leadership position in pharmaceuticals, Hewlett-Packard's reputation for quality, and the Xerox commitment to customer service have been built over many years and overshadow individual product successes (and occasional failures).[6]

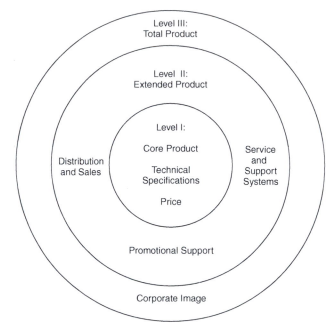

FIGURE 8.1. The High-Tech Product Positioning Model

SEGMENTATION STRATEGY DEVELOPMENT

Marketing strategy was touched upon in Chapter 3 (the marketing planning section). Segmentation strategy is the process whereby a firm maximizes the marketing controllables (the Four Ps) toward satisfying a target market's needs. Marketing strategy recognizes the dynamics of markets, and the objectives, resources, and "personality" of a company. Personality means the company's business character/culture (its organizational philosophy and management style) and the importance of people functions in the marketing plan.

Hence, a master marketing program must mesh with your company's business style and be appropriate for the firm given its present situation. Marketing is not a business function to be undertaken by only the marketing researchers, advertising department, or sales force. It is an ongoing series of activities that permeates all levels of the company, from president to part-time help. Similarly, all levels of the company must be apprised of appropriate strategies or tactics relevant to their areas of responsibility.

Successful segmentation strategy consists of two phases: first, market niches/segments must be found and pursued (this three-step process was just described). This strategic position activates the overall direction the company will follow. Next, primary and secondary marketing mix elements must be reviewed, formulated, or revised. These are the weapons used to win the "marketing war."

In designing marketing strategies for a target group, three broad business areas must be carefully analyzed. They are internal and external marketing factors, and customer needs. The Environmental Scorecard (Table 8.2) is a useful worksheet for rating and comparing the strengths and weaknesses of many corporate and industry-related issues that impact business segmentation. Customer needs must consider how segments are defined based on the typical firmographic and behavioral segmentation dimensions and variables; product uses and usage patterns (*note:* since consumptive measures frequently are dependent variables, it is advisable to separate out this base); present levels of product satisfaction; etc.

Bringing "life" to the segmentation analysis is the function of strategic implementation. No longer are we concerned with "what if" questions—as Nike says, "Just do it." Successful implementation of prescribed marketing strategy requires the talents of many professionals. Marketing analysts, researchers, planners, strategists, advertising and public relations personnel, the sales team, consultants, and marketing managers must all work in concert to accomplish corporate objectives. In addition, the marketing department must interface with corporate management to ensure that strategic thrusts are compatible with organizational policies and values. Assuming all systems are go, a "master implementation switch" is turned on, and plans are ready to become actions.

The ultimate objective of the segmentation study is to assist your firm in increasing its number of customers, and in turn your revenues and profits. This can be accomplished in one of three ways: attracting nonusers to your product, increasing the usage of existing customers, and/or developing new markets.

TABLE 8.2. The Environmental Scorecard

Internal Situation	Strength Weakness Neutral Factor	+ – 0	External Situation	Strength Weakness Neutral Factor	+ – 0
Resources			*Your market*		
People			Size		
Financial			Potential		
Facilities			Growth trends		
Equipment			Homogeneity		
Computers			Opportunities		
Other (list)			Problems		
Past performance			*Competition*		
Corporate			Number		
Division			Strength		
SBU			Market structure		
Product line			Threats		
Product			*Environmental*		
Constraints			Economic		
Objectives			Firmographics		
Commitment			Legal		
Policies (list)			Natural/physical		
Current marketing strategies			Political		
Product			Technological		
Pricing					
Promotion					
Distribution					
E-business					

Are actual results meeting expectations? Probably not. In most business situations, there will be a number of unforeseen occurrences impacting the product market—some favorable, some unfavorable. The goal is to maximize your opportunities and circumvent your threats. This is where the essential, but often overlooked, evaluation process takes over. For top effectiveness, control systems should be built prior to implementing marketing strategy. This mechanism leads to quick detection of potential roadblocks and advantageous situations. Implementation and control is a major part of a sound overall marketing program.

The Target Market Strategy Worksheet (Segmentation Skillbuilder 8) provides a summary model for identifying key strategic issues and capitalizing on them. An in-depth strategic plan is the recommended next step. You want to produce a consistent, information-backed document with synergism created among all of its components. Such a project can be readily implemented and monitored for performance.

BUSINESS SEGMENTATION AND THE MARKETING MIX

Next, we will briefly explore how segmentation impacts the core elements of a marketing strategy (the Four Ps). While e-commerce issues are not specifically reviewed in this section, they should be integrated into all facets of marketing activity in the organization. (A good overview of the e-marketing mix and today's business challenges is provided in a recent article by Kalyanam and McIntyre.[7])

Product Strategy

In segmentation studies, the customers' views toward the product are the driving force in shaping appropriate product decisions. In developing these strategies, a firm must analyze all of the goods or services it offers. This includes individual product items/brands, product lines, and the product mix the business handles. In segmentation strategy planning, we are more concerned with specific product units or families of products than entire product classes, markets, or industry sales volume. Factors that impact product strategy decisions include the nature of the product, the product life cycle, the classification of goods, product policies, and the role of product differentiation.

The nature of the product refers to the basic characteristics of the good or service. Some important product questions to ask are listed in Box 8.2. Once these issues are resolved, the firm has a good understanding of the intricacies of the product, its applications, and the market it is competing in—a key toward strategy formulation.

Life cycles provide another useful tool for analyzing products prior to strategy development. Like people, industries and products

SEGMENTATION SKILLBUILDER 8:
TARGET MARKET STRATEGY WORKSHEET

Segment Name/Brief Description:

Opportunities:

1.

2.

3.

Threats:

1.

2.

3.

Goals:

- Marketing:
- Financial:

Overall Marketing Strategy:

Marketing Mix Strategies

	Present Strategy	Recommended Strategies	Potential Impact
Product			
Promotion			
Pricing			
Distribution			
E-Commerce			

Marketing Mix Tactics

	Present Tactics	Recommended Tactics	Potential Impact
Product			
Promotion			
Pricing			
Distribution			
E-Commerce			

Evaluation/Control Measures:

BOX 8.2. The Nature of the Product

- What type of product is it?
- What is it primarily used for?
- Are there any other applications for the product?
- Who uses the product?
- Why do they use it?
- What benefits are customers seeking?
- Is there anything customers or potential customers do not like about the product? Why?
- Is the product branded?
- Does it have any other favorable proprietary positions (i.e., patents, copyrights, and/or trademarks)?
- How is the product manufactured?
- How is the product distributed?
- How is it promoted?
- How does your Web site sell the product?
- How is it priced?
- What is the product's past performance (sales figures, strengths, and weaknesses)?
- Does the company produce any related products?
- What is the competitive environment like?

---

have an aging process. This five-phase life cycle consists of birth, growth, maturity, decline, and death. It is important to assess where your industry is, and where it is headed.

Also, determine where your product is in its life cycle. At the introductory and early growth stages of a market, products will appeal to innovators and the early adopters. As the industry develops and matures, competition will intensify and new segmentation strategies will be needed to find a niche in the marketplace. Finally, at the decline stage, the customer pool has been severely depleted, and the remaining market segments must be nurtured and cultivated for efforts to remain profitable.

The classification of goods framework divides industrial products into groupings of similar products based on their inherent qualities or characteristics. Industrial goods can be classified into capital purchases (such as buildings or heavy equipment), tools and other equipment, raw materials, parts and materials, supplies, and industrial services.

Product policies relate to the firm's business mission and operating philosophy. These are constraints or guideposts that govern product decisions. Product policies serve to limit product choices in a number of strategic areas. The first consideration is the markets to compete in and the broad product offerings to compete with. Other product policies can relate to the company's product testing program (planning efforts, research and development, and test marketing), new product policies (a product innovator or imitator), product mix decisions (including branding and product line extensions or deletions), as well as packaging, warranties, and service.

The four product factors we have explored so far provide some direction for a market segmentation program—adapting the product or service to meet the unique needs of selected target markets. In some cases, however, product differentiation—emphasizing the product differences/features rather than the customer needs (if the needs for a product are basically the same)—is the more important marketing strategy.

An overall product strategy must still be formulated. Each of the five areas discussed can play a key role in this process. Astute marketers realize that product decisions are closely linked to the other marketing controllables (promotion, pricing, and distribution). Based on an analysis of the product factors, product-oriented strategies emerge. These might include the introduction, modification, or elimination of products.

Modification can be minor or major. The objective is to reposition, reformulate, or repackage the goods or services to appeal to new segments of the market or strengthen the firm's market position with existing segments. Another option, at times viable, is no change. If the analysis indicates that the present product mix is strong, strategic marketing changes may be called for in other functional areas. In addition to prescribed overhauls for overall product strategy, sometimes dozens of tactical product decisions may need to be made to fine-tune a company's product offerings.

Promotional Strategy

Companies can reach and persuade their target markets by using a mix of traditional promotional elements (advertising, personal selling, publicity, and sales promotion) and targeted promotional tools (databases, direct marketing, and the Internet). Integrated marketing communications (IMC) means communicating a consistent and synergistic message across all media (one look, one voice)—this conveys value to targeted audiences. Research found that 62 percent of B2B companies had fully coordinated IMC programs, 19 percent were mostly coordinated, and 19 percent were partly or not coordinated.[8] Next, we will review the traditional promotional practices in business markets in further detail (interested readers should consult specialized references to get a better handle on the newer promotional options).

Personal selling is characterized by face-to-face communication about a good or service. It is a deceptively important promotional strategy, particularly in business markets. In the United States, more is spent in this area than for advertising. Selling is where the actual dollars (or yen, deutsche marks, pounds, francs, etc.) change hands in product, service, and government markets. Good selling is matching customer needs to a firm's offerings. If this is accomplished, a sale is made, a satisfied customer established, and potential long-term relationships are begun.

The beauty of personal selling is that its objective parallels that of market segmentation—tailoring products to meet customers' desires. The one major weakness plaguing this promotional approach is its high costs. (Table 8.3 summarizes cost data for business sales calls.) Given this limitation, the other mass promotional techniques can be employed to generate highly qualified inquiries/leads to make personal selling more efficient (hence, improve the closing ratio).

Advertising is paid, nonpersonal communication of ideas, goods, or services by an identified sponsor. It is a dynamic, interesting, and at times glamorous field that is often misunderstood by the public. Advertising is also a very complex area with many interrelated components affecting its overall business impact (e.g., media options,

TABLE 8.3. SM&M's Cost-per-Call Survey, 1999

Sales Approach	Cost per Sales Call (in U.S. dollars)
Value-added—stresses solution over price	189
Transactional—price emphasis	84
Products customized to client needs	164
Product and price emphasis	156
Service companies	242
Industrial manufacturers	202

Source: "The Cost of Doing Business," *Sales and Marketing Management Magazine,* September 1999, p. 56. Adapted from data provided by the Canadian Professional Sales Association, <www.cpsa.com/Publications/Gui/Html/WeekofSept13_1999.asp>.

budgets, media selection and scheduling, message preparation, the role of the advertising agency, and measurement techniques).

Depending on a company's promotional focus, advertising can span the gamut from being virtually nonexistent to being a major factor in determining a firm's success or lack thereof. Generally speaking, advertising plays a support function to selling, sales promotion, and databases in business markets. From a segmentation perspective, advertising can be an excellent, but not inexpensive, means of reaching out to the firm's most likely prospects, its target markets.

Successful advertising calls for investing your dollars wisely. Advertising expenditures should be allocated to those media vehicles which can best deliver target markets. Scores of different media can be used. (One advertising professional claimed that more than 14,000 choices exist!) Obviously, most of these media are obscure, impractical, or unimportant. For simplicity, media can be divided into three major classes:

1. Broadcast—radio, television, film, and other electronic media
2. Print—newspapers and many types of trade periodicals
3. Other media—Internet, catalogs, direct mail, directories, outdoor and transit billboards, specialty advertising, etc.

In addition to the media classifications, there is an abundance of media vehicles to choose from. The more highly selective the advertising, the better for reaching designated market segments—this minimizes audience waste (going after suspects rather than prospects). In addition to media considerations, creative and copy platforms must be developed in meeting segment needs.

Publicity or public relations (PR) is unpaid news about a company, employee, product, or service. Unlike advertising, which is company sponsored, publicity is placed by an outside organization and is perceived as being more objective. Excluding PR initiation costs, publicity is free promotion, and its exposure can provide a most favorable response to the firm. In addition to targeted media vehicles used in a well-executed publicity campaign, speaking engagements, written materials, and special events are typically featured. Accountants, financial planners, lawyers, and management consultants are examples of professionals who have recognized the value of publicity as a new business generator.

Sales promotion augments selling and advertising efforts, such as trade shows/exhibits, product demonstrations, displays, samples, price incentives, contests, and other special promotional activities. The underlying question to answer prior to the use of any and all promotional strategies and tactics is, "Is it right for the market segment you are trying to attract?"

Pricing Strategy

How much should you charge your customers for your product? This question is one of pricing strategy. Setting prices for your goods or services is not a simple issue. Many marketing and financial factors affect this decision. Financial costs (e.g., markups, margins, paybacks, etc.) are important when setting price, but other marketing factors must be considered. These include the firm's operating philosophy and the image it wishes to convey, the competitive situation, other external factors, the target market the company is pursuing, customer price expectations, product factors, promotional strategies employed, and distribution channels used. Price/quality trade-offs may exist or be perceived by target markets (some customers feel that because a product is more expensive, it is a better product—this may or may not be true).

Pricing is not a unidimensional variable. For many products, the price is a package composed of several elements. In business situations, the price may be affected by credit/lease terms, shipping expenses, trade discounts, price incentives, and/or service fees. The bottom line is that price setting is not something to be taken lightly. Like other strategic aspects of the marketing plan, careful research is vital in this area.

As Figure 8.2 illustrates, pricing strategy must relate to a target market's level of price sensitivity. Since buyers do not value all product attributes equally, identifiable market segments (and customers) are attracted to goods and services at varying price points. Hotels and airlines are masters at price point segmentation.

Although we seldom think of pricing as a major part of a segmentation study, this is not always the case. Johnson & Johnson's Cordis division is the market leader in products for the diagnostic coronary and peripheral markets, supplying a large percentage of all coronary catheters used worldwide. In one segmentation research project, cardiologists and other physicians were queried as to their preferences for various features and pricing levels for a proposed new medical device.

Ideally, pricing strategy should be based on an in-depth analysis of your company's marketing situation. Specifically, a firm will take one of four directions:

1. *Beat their price:* This strategy depends on high volume, since low price implies operating on low margins.
2. *Meet their price:* This competitive pricing strategy recognizes market forces. In this instance, the firm competes on some nonprice issues in an attempt to differentiate itself from the other firms. This can include having a better product, an improved image or reputation, offering postsale servicing, etc.
3. *Do not compete on price:* If a higher-price strategy is being used, the firm must provide additional benefits to its customers or convince them that they are purchasing "top quality." High

prices may be justified where there is limited competition, high costs associated with new product development, exclusive products offered, or limited consumer resistance.

4. *Retreat due to price:* In some circumstances, the firm may not have the economies of scale or other operating efficiencies to compete profitably in a market situation. In this case, the recommended strategy might be to cut your losses and get out of that market and allocate those resources toward other more attractive market opportunities.

Distribution Strategy

As an integral part of the marketing mix, channels of distribution (an often neglected controllable) need to be periodically examined. A marketing channel is an exchange pathway through which goods are moved, flowing from the production point to intermediaries, and finally to the ultimate consumers. A channel might include a manufacturer, one or more middlemen, retailers, and customers, although shorter channels are evident in many business situations (e.g., buying direct from manufacturers or wholesalers via a Web site). Table 8.4 identifies the customer focus for the segmentation analysis in industrial markets.

While marketing channel decisions tend to be well entrenched (it is a relatively fixed marketing variable), present strategies should be analyzed to determine if they are the most efficient ones possible. Sometimes minor changes such as using a new supplier can have a fa-

---

PRICE CEILING

Price Point 1—Segment A
Price Point 2—Segment B
Price Point 3—Segment C
Price Point 4—Segment X

PRICE FLOOR

FIGURE 8.2. Price-Based Target Marketing

vorable impact on a company's distribution program. Some distribution strategy options for the firm include the following:

- *Long versus short channels:* A long channel uses several intermediaries to handle storage, sorting, transportation, promotion, and related functions. The other extreme is the short channel, which implies a direct relationship.
- *Wide versus narrow channels:* If the objective is to get the product into as many outlets as possible, a wide channel strategy is employed. Building an extensive distribution network is necessary if mass-marketing tactics are used. Narrower channels recognize the value of market segmentation. One example of this channel strategy might be to establish relationships with exclusive distributors that are territory-based (U.S. regions or countries).
- *Push versus pull strategies:* If the product is promoted to other channel members (manufacturers to wholesalers to retailers, for example), a push strategy is used. Grocery product manufacturers promote their goods to consumers (end users) to stimulate intermediate demand—a pull strategy.
- *Imitate versus innovate:* Traditional channels of distribution are the obvious, safe, and uncreative approach. Many times this is the way to go. However, if a new or modified channel can be found, a competitive edge is likely to arise. In our new economy, distribution channels may be found in *marketspace* (the Internet) as well as the marketplace. The need for partnering and creating value chain networks is also a desirable approach for twenty-first-century companies.

These strategies are polar extremes. Not everything in life and in marketing is black and white. Varying degrees of gray also occur. Therefore, a channel may be shorter or longer, wider or narrower, etc. Combinations of push and pull and imitation and innovation may also be required. In addition, several of these channel strategy options may be happening simultaneously (e.g., short, narrow channels).

TABLE 8.4. Who Is Your Customer?

Seller	Buyer			
	Manufacturer	Wholesaler	Retailer	Service Firm
Manufacturer	X	X	X	X
Wholesaler		X	X	X
Retailer			X	X
Service firm	X	X	X	X

Note: X denotes a typical customer. Although there is occasional upward channel movement in business markets (for example, a large retailer selling to a small wholesaler), virtually all marketing efforts are directed at the same channel level (such as manufacturer to manufacturer) or downward (such as manufacturer to wholesaler).

TARGET MARKET STRATEGY: AN APPLICATION

Rather than taking a bits-and-pieces approach to strategy formation, think of the gestalt (holistic) approach to segmentation-based marketing decision making. Use profiles of selected target markets to predict and understand your customers' purchase behavior. Furthermore, such insights are essential for developing realistic and responsive segment-specific strategies to maximize marketing performance (e.g., sales and profits). A company specializing in home improvement, such as Home Depot, can benefit by knowing its customers (contractors) inside and out and offering them a marketing program that best satisfies their needs (see Table 8.5).

SUMMARY

The segmentation study is complete; prospective target markets have surfaced, been evaluated, and selected. With methodological issues behind us, segmentation strategy takes center stage. By understanding customer behavior, choosing the right user segments, and designing unique positioning strategies, your firm can carve a profitable niche in today's highly competitive global marketplace.

TABLE 8.5. The Contractor Segment

Behavioral Segmentation Variable	Operationalization of Key Variables
User situation	Professional tradesmen, project work-for-hires
User profile	Carpenters, general contractors, electricians, painters, plumbers, freelance handymen, etc.
Knowledge level	Experts in their trades
Motivations	Earn a living, do a good job
Marketing program	Quality goods, product depth, value-added services, advance orders, separate checkout areas, easy credit terms, professional discounts, volume discounts

Sound segmentation strategy originates from researching customer needs and your internal (corporate) and external (industry) marketing environments. The proper mix of the Four Ps leads to market success. Product strategy considers the nature of the product, its life cycle, goods classifications, product policies, and differentiation. Targeted pricing is based on your firm's operating philosophy/image, competition, cost, and customer expectations. The promotional blend combines databases, advertising, personal selling, publicity, and sales promotion to reach prime prospects efficiently and effectively. Place (distribution) decisions relate to channel length, width, focus, and innovativeness.

Realize that successful segmentation/target market strategy is a systematic, integrative, and synergistic process and that evaluation and control completes the market-driven cycle. In Chapter 9, we will explain how to create a long-term, internal marketing environment conducive to maximizing the value of customer analysis as well as some segmentation challenges faced by business marketers.

Chapter 9

Enhancing Segmentation's Value

Take time to deliberate, but when the time for action has arrived,
stop thinking and go in.

Napoleon Bonaparte (1815)

The segmentation study is analyzed; target markets have been
identified. Methodological issues are behind us; strategy has been developed. There is still important work to be completed—specifically,
building a marketing organization capable of effectively and efficiently planning and executing segmentation findings. This chapter
addresses this key implementation issue. We will examine how to
create a customer-driven organizational culture, a game plan for initiating needed segmentation activities and projects, the benefits of a
segmentation audit, and segmentation challenges for business marketers.

CREATING A SEGMENTATION-DRIVEN
ORGANIZATION

A successful customer-centric marketing program can be initiated
by using three stages: (1) understand, commit, and plan segmentation
analyses (Chapters 1 through 3); (2) conduct the study (Chapters 4
through 7); and (3) develop and implement the segmentation-based
strategy (Chapters 8 and 9 and case studies). This process is shown in
Box 9.1.

Realize that segmentation can reward your company with some or
all of these riches: improved prospecting methods and sales closing

---

BOX 9.1. A Segmentation Framework

Segmentation Planning

- Understand market definition/segmentation
- Commit to a segmentation-based marketing strategy
- Use segmentation planning and research guidelines

Segmenting Markets

- Define the market geographically
- Assess firmographic (business demographics) variables
- Analyze product usage patterns
- Incorporate organizational psychographics, as applicable
- Benefit from benefit segmentation techniques
- Use the nested approach for business segmentation
- Conduct the study

Segmentation Implementation

- Develop a segmentation-based target market strategy
- Create a segmentation-driven corporate culture
- Monitor and evaluate segmentation performance

---

ratios, new customers, better customers (a segment of the market desired), more satisfied customers (products closely aligned to customer needs and wants), long-term customer relationships, increased sales and profits, new business opportunities, and improved market share and share of customer measures.

While this process may take considerable time, resources, and effort, a segmentation-led company builds on well-conceived research and plans differentiated strategies to strive for market dominance in specialized markets. Business and technology companies often have a product orientation rather than a marketing mind-set. Successful segmentation strategies require a strong customer commitment. Business Segmentation Insight 9 examines how the unique challenges present in high-tech organizations impact the market segmentation process.

BUSINESS SEGMENTATION INSIGHT 9: HOW HIGH-TECH BUSINESS CULTURES IMPACT SEGMENTATION STRATEGY

Most high-technology companies are primarily led and staffed by technical managers with backgrounds and educational training in engineering, production, research and development, or the sciences. These individuals are valuable for developing new technologies, products, and business applications and relate well to technical-minded customers.

As Workman explains, many high-tech products are modular and flexible and can be configured for different applications to meet the needs of different market segments. Customization is an important value-added activity since products must often mesh with other firm's components, software, and peripherals.[1]

While the technology-oriented culture is a breeding ground for innovation for start-up and growing companies, marketing functions typically assume a subservient position in high-tech organizations. In the growth and maturity stages, marketing plays an essential role in finding new opportunities and protecting established target markets. Since there are few "pure" marketers in the company, product and marketing managers generally have had limited academic training or marketing experience relevant to market segmentation.

In corporate training programs I conducted for Bayer, Hewlett-Packard, Intel, Motorola, Novartis, and other companies, many participants (including MBAs with technical undergraduate degrees) have commented that they learned more about segmentation in a one-day session than during the course of their university education. Therefore, I strongly urge top management to elevate the market segmentation function and marketing management activities in high-tech organizations.

In the past few years, I am pleased to notice positive strides as progressive organizations are now creating positions such as market segmentation or segment manager, manager of new business opportunities, customer relationship manager, and related new job titles. This implies that the message is getting out—it is the *customer* not the corporation that sets the true agenda for exchange and change in business.

Ideally, market segmentation managers should work closely with researchers, strategists, and consultants on the study. This approach provides practical information to today's hard-hitting questions. It also precludes possible misunderstandings at a later date. Regular meetings and two-way communication between management (including upper-level management) and the project team leads to higher-quality segmentation results. The following eight segmentation management guidelines provide overall direction for maximizing segmentation's value in your marketing plan:

1. Integrate segmentation with all other marketing management activities.
2. Be actively involved in the segmentation program.
3. Have realistic expectations about the value of segmentation in your company.
4. Listen to the results.
5. Dare to be different.
6. Request frequent updates and projections.
7. Get professional assistance when necessary.
8. Treat segmentation analysis as an investment.

STRATEGIC SEGMENTATION AND IMPLEMENTATION CONSIDERATIONS

The current level of sophistication of a firm's segmentation programs and processes should be assessed. Business marketers and managers need to understand the strategic importance of segmentation, models and frameworks that are practical and easy to use, the value of market research, the financial costs associated with target marketing, how to measure performance, and areas where organizational improvements are necessary (e.g., personnel, resources, techniques, etc.).

According to Jenkins and McDonald, the market segmentation function can be evaluated based on two dimensions: customer-driven and organizational integration. This results in a 2 × 2 matrix consisting of four possible segmentation archetypes (see Figure 9.1). While

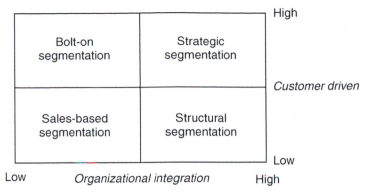

FIGURE 9.1. Types of Segmentation Organizations (*Source:* Mark Jenkins and Malcolm McDonald, "Market Segmentation: Organizational Archetypes and Research Agendas," *European Journal of Marketing,* 31[1], 1997, pp. 17-32.)

strategic segmentation is clearly the desired state and the focus of our book—i.e., a company rates highly on both dimensions—three other segmentation structures are commonly found. Sales-based segmentation fares poorly on both customer focus and organizational integration; generally segmentation is limited to sales territory analysis. Structural segmenters do a good job of integrating segmentation throughout the organization but are not customer driven; typically, they practice product-level segmentation. Finally, bolt-on segmentation characterizes an organization that uses customer data effectively for promotional purposes but does little else to integrate segmentation thinking throughout the organization.[2]

Professors Sally Dibb and Lyndon Simkin of the United Kingdom have studied industrial segmentation implementation issues for more than a decade. Their empirical, case, and conceptual research has clarified more than two dozen problem areas regarding segmentation *infrastructure* (e.g., no MIS in place, company resistant to new ideas, lack of customer focus), *process* (lack of right personnel to undertake segmentation, poor understanding of segmentation process, role of corporate strategic planning, etc.), and *operations* (ineffective communication, inflexibility in the distribution system, inadequate budgeting for implementation, etc.) faced by business marketers. A general prescription for remedying these segmentation shortcomings is summarized in Table 9.1. Based on Dibb and Simkin's work, Segmentation Skillbuilder 9 poses nine key questions on implementation.

Dibb and Simkin's three-stage now, future, and how approach is an insightful segmentation planning tool for business marketers. According to the authors, the *now* is the core analyses that need to be conducted regarding the existing marketing situation, the internal and external environments, general trends, customer desires and buying behavior, competitive strategy, and product management. The *future* is the strategic thinking required about new segmentation criteria and dimensions, segment opportunities, and target market positioning. The *how* is the segmentation implementation mandate and assesses the Four Ps, resources and scheduling, and ongoing requirements (i.e., product development, marketing research, training, evaluating performance, and communications).[4]

TABLE 9.1. Overcoming Segmentation Implementation Barriers

Infrastructure (prior to undertaking segmentation)	Procedural (during the segmentation process)	Operational (facilitates segmentation implementation)
Review available marketing intelligence	Specify sequential steps for segmentation process	Identify key internal and external audiences
Identify relevant people and skills	Identify skill gaps, find consultants, provide training	Designate internal champion(s) to communicate segmentation findings to key players
Get top management buy-in	Prioritize information gaps, collect data, create/update MIS	Devise necessary changes to organizational culture/systems
Plan and facilitate communication channels	Have regular debriefings of analyses, ideas	Reallocate personnel and resources based on segment findings/plan
Earmark required resources	Review ongoing fit with corporate strategy	Specify schedule and responsibilities to roll out segment solutions
Develop an internal orientation of segmentation objectives		Create mechanism for monitoring segment performance

Source: Adapted from Sally Dibb and Lyndon Simkin, "Market Segmentation: Diagnosing and Treating the Barriers," *Industrial Marketing Management,* 30, 2001, pp. 609-625.

With this segmentation implementation primer in place, it is helpful to observe the specific types of research activities that need to be performed, by whom, and how long they will take to complete (see Table 9.2). Next, we examine how a segmentation audit can be used by progressive companies.

THE SEGMENTATION AUDIT

Every firm should periodically place itself under the microscope. One of the best ways of assessing your current marketing situation is to conduct a market segmentation audit. This is not an easy task, however. As Hal W. Goetsch, former director of marketing for the American Mar-

TABLE 9.2. Segmentation Research Initiatives

Segmentation Activity	Responsibility	Timeline (estimated)
Commit to developing a segmentation-led company	Top management	1-2 weeks
Conduct a visioning session	Top management, marketing management, external facilitator (desirable)	2-3 weeks
Segmentation training, basic concepts	Marketing management, consultant	2-4 weeks
Segmentation training, customized	Marketing management, consultant(s)	4-6 weeks
Market profile	Marketing researcher, consultant	3-4 weeks (internal), 4-6 weeks (external)
Segmentation audit	Consultant	1 month
Segmentation research, specialized project (e.g., new product)	Marketing management, consultant	2-3 months
Segmentation research, major project (e.g., business unit)	Marketing management, consultant	3-4 months
Segmentation research program	Top management, marketing management, marketing organization, consultants	6 months to 2 years

**SEGMENTATION SKILLBUILDER 9: SEGMENTATION
IMPLEMENTATION QUESTIONS**

1. Is management committed to the process?
2. Are lines of communication open throughout the organization?
3. Do you have a management information system (MIS) in place for gathering marketing intelligence?
4. Do you have sufficient marketing data and internal consensus for logically grouping market subsets?
5. Does the chosen segmentation scheme fit the organization's mission and strategic planning initiatives?
6. Do you have managerial support to provide appropriate personnel and adequate finances for the segmentation initiative?
7. Is communication strategy in place for informing both internal and external constituencies?
8. Are the right people in place and committed to operationalizing the segmentation scheme?
9. Has management shown long-term commitment to segmentation rollout and monitoring?

Source: Prepared by Scott A. Anderson, Assistant Professor of Marketing, Buena Vista University, Storm Lake, Iowa. (*Note:* Questions 1 through 3 relate to segmentation infrastructure, questions 4 through 6 refer to segmentation processes, and questions 7 through 9 focus on segmentation operations/implementation.)

keting Association explained, marketing audits can present problems for a company when it attempts to administer them internally. He stated:

> Even when a conscientious effort is made to see the situation objectively, the focus can be blurred by tradition, unquestioned procedures, personalities, manipulated programs, corporate politics, indifference, or laziness. Too often the picture is faulty because facts are missing, guesses are not reliable, or important elements of the marketing environment have been ignored or overlooked.[5]

To resolve this problem, the audit should be administered by an outside marketing consultant to minimize bias and maximize objectivity. An effective segmentation audit will gather information about your current marketing efforts and, more important, analyze the marketing health of your firm—similar to the ways a medical checkup assesses one's physical well-being. Strengths and weaknesses of the company are readily identified; the aim is to capitalize on the former, while rectifying the latter.

What types of organizations can benefit most from a marketing/segmentation audit? Although this planning review should be periodically conducted for all firms, it is particularly helpful for production and technically oriented companies, troubled divisions, high-performing business units, young companies, and nonprofit organizations.[6]

Goetsch's overall marketing audit questions for a business provide a good starting point for undertaking a detailed segmentation analysis. The audit must be modified, however, to meet the information-gathering needs of a particular firm and industry. For example, an adapted audit consisting of thirty-one key segmentation issues in six marketing functional areas is summarized in Box 9.2. This instrument was personally administered to several marketing executives at Intel's OEM Systems Division. The output of this planning and diagnostic tool was the identification of some significant marketing problems/issues, proposed solutions, and ideas for pursuing viable niche

---

BOX 9.2. The Segmentation Audit

I. Sales History
1. How do sales break down within the product line?
2. Do you know where sales are coming from—segments and customer classification?
3. Which products/markets/segments are not meeting potential? Why?

II. Marketing Commitment
1. Is formal marketing planning ingrained with all marketing management?

(continued)

(continued)

    2. Do you implement a marketing plan, set objectives, measure performance, and adjust for deviation?
    3. Is the marketing plan largely based on segmentation findings?

III. Marketing Environment

    1. What major developments and trends pose opportunities or threats to the company?
    2. What actions have been taken in response to these developments and trends?
    3. What major changes are occurring in technology? What is the company's position in these technologies?
    4. What are the competitors' positions in the market (strengths and weaknesses, strategies, etc.)?
    5. What is happening to market size, growth rates, profits, and related market considerations?

IV. Market Segments

    1. In your view, what are the major market segments?
    2. How do different customer segments make their buying decisions?
    3. Who are potential customers for your product?
    4. Are segments identified, measured, and monitored?
    5. Are any small but profitable segments overlooked?
    6. How do you presently segment the market?
    7. Is the present segmentation approach effective?
    8. Have you developed detailed customer profiles for major market segments?
    9. Should the company contract or withdraw from any business segment? What would be the short- and long-run consequences of this decision?
    10. Are market segment definitions based on research?

V. Product

    1. What are the product line objectives?
    2. Is the company well organized to gather, generate, and screen new product ideas?
    3. Does the company carry out adequate product and market research before launching new products?
    4. Is there a well-defined program to weed out unprofitable products and add new ones?

> 5. Is there a systematic liaison with R&D and other key departments in the company?
> VI. Marketing Management
>   1. Are marketing activities optimally structured along functional, product, end user, and territorial lines?
>   2. Are marketing resources allocated optimally to market segments, products, and territories?
>   3. Is an adequate, accurate, and timely marketing intelligence/marketing information system in place?
>   4. Is the marketing research being effectively used by company decision makers?
>   5. Does management regularly analyze the profitability of products, markets, territories, and related issues?
>
> *Source:* Based on ideas from Hal W. Goetsch, "Conduct a Comprehensive Marketing Audit to Improve Marketing Planning," *Marketing News,* March 18, 1983, Section 2, p. 14; and from Philip Kotler, *Marketing Management: Analysis, Planning, Implementation, and Control,* Seventh Edition (Englewood Cliffs, NJ: Prentice-Hall, 1991), pp. 726-728.

opportunities. Table 9.3 highlights some key findings from this segmentation audit.

TWENTY-FIRST-CENTURY B2B SEGMENTATION: A LOOK BACK, A LOOK AHEAD

In the second edition of my market segmentation book (published in 1994), I offered readers my thoughts as to where segmentation was headed by the year 2000. These were not meant to be major, earth-shattering relevations since they were basically an extension of what was developing in the early 1990s. Rather, these insights were designed to provide guidance to marketers as to what to expect over the next few years.

Segmentation Then

A look back shows that five of the original six prognostications relevant to business market segmentation have gained prominence. (*Note:* one prediction focused solely on consumer markets.) These

TABLE 9.3. Segmentation Audit Findings—Intel's OEM Systems

Marketing Deficiencies Identified	Marketing Recommendations	Niche/Segmentation Opportunities
Engineering driven	Become leading-edge marketer as well as leading-edge manufacturer.	Marketing input must transition from nominal to powerful; segmentation insights should guide engineering.
Lack of marketing information	Marketing research function/department needs to be established.	Hire market segmentation manager and a marketing visionary.
Need to redefine business mission and objectives	Work with Santa Clara components division on this.	Provide more end user solutions—complete/integrated systems.
Need to determine how separate or together are OMSO, OPO, and DTO (SBUs)	Reconcile the roles of OMSO, OPO, and DTO within the OSD business.	OPO only in one segment; need to branch out.
Defining markets/segments where to compete	Explore and attack niche markets.	Strengthen presence in government sector, oil industry, low-power-consumption products, low-cost input/output products, software, clone manufacturers, high-volume end users.
No widely accepted view of what segmentation is in the organization	Get outside marketing input—consultants, professors, professional seminars.	Develop companywide segmentation philosophy, models, and processes.
Need to improve vertical market capabilities	Understand segment needs.	Elevators, power plants, ultrasound machines, etc.
Products not always reflective of customer needs	Conduct product-specific segmentation research prior to product development.	Spend less time writing proposals and more time interacting with customers.
Conservative, generic product plans	Build on sustainable differentiating advantages.	Unlike Motorola, sell front-end tools and languages, aggressively attack niche markets.
Unfocused sales force	Internal sales reorganization—need for more than one sales force?	Develop customer-centric sales approach.

were as follows: entering the era of micro/niche marketing, increased use of computer technology, global segmentation, private-sector segmentation providers to gain in importance, and greater acceptance of segmentation by organizations.

A classic work on market segmentation was written by Jerry (Yoram) Wind about twenty-five years ago. In this influential article (arguably the second most important scholarly segmentation article behind Smith, see note 3, Chapter 1), Wind acknowledges that business markets are in need of further study since most segmentation efforts are consumer based. He concludes his in-depth treatise of the segmentation design and research process with a set of twelve methodological, theoretical, and strategic needs for investigation. While academics and market researchers have made progress in the first two areas (research and theory), Wind's strategic issues are worth revisiting a quarter of a century later. His five strategic priorities are briefly summarized as follows:

1. New conceptualization of the segmentation problem
2. Discovering and implementing new variables as segmentation bases
3. Accumulating knowledge on successful segmentation bases for products, situations, and markets
4. Exploring alternative approaches to translate segmentation findings into marketing strategies
5. Studies of the companies that were successful (or unsuccessful) in implementing segmentation strategies[7]

In *Handbook of Market Segmentation: Strategic Targeting for Business and Technology Firms,* Third Edition, I have carefully considered these critical points via a framework of segmentation planning, selecting relevant business segmentation bases, and target market strategy. Among the "big" questions business marketers should be able to answer more completely (and segmentation bases to consult) include these:

- Where do I find my customers (geographics)?
- What are the organizational characteristics of customers (firmographics)?

- What are they buying (usage)?
- What are their needs and desires (benefits)?
- What are the key buying discriminators (purchasing behavior/organizational psychographics)?

Segmentation Now

In the decade since the last edition of the book was published, a number of driving marketing forces have occurred that have greatly impacted business segmentation. These include the increased attention on segment-of-one marketing, a focus on relationship marketing/customer retention, buyers seeking value and benefits over price, the Internet explosion, the NAICS, a transition into a services and an information- based economy, and a proliferation of strategic partnerships/business alliances. These issues have been addressed to varying degrees in this book.

Realize that successful market segmentation initiatives are strategic (not short term); there are no magic formulas or seven-point plans that will work in all cases. In one long-term segmentation project I was involved in with a major medical device manufacturer, we developed four unique research studies over a three-year period to assess the myriad of challenges presented by management objectives, fierce competition, changing technologies, personnel capabilities, customer wants, and so forth.

I recommend that business marketers first objectively evaluate their level of segmentation sophistication. Build on what is working and add pieces to the segmentation puzzle for areas that have been neglected or are in need of improvement. It is much better to go slow and "get it right" rather than attempt to take on more than the organization can handle. The segmentation audit and/or the nested approach exercise (see Segmentation Skillbuilder 7) are superb building blocks for initiating new and improved segmentation programs and processes in high-tech and industrial companies.

Creativity in market analysis is also highly encouraged. While most marketers and managers feel comfortable with so-called accepted or recognized industry segmentations, generally these are product based rather than customer focused. Seldom do they provide a firm with a competitive advantage. In segmentation training programs and consulting engagements, I encourage participants and clients to think about throwing out the prevailing thinking and build original, proprietary segmentation models. Innovative segmentation bases, frameworks, or multistage models that "break the mold" help the firm find market segments and niches that the competition has overlooked.

Segmentation benchmarking in related industries/sectors can be insightful, too. As an example, Nortel was advised to benchmark Texas Instruments' segmentation activities in the Dallas–Fort Worth area. Both companies were of similar size; are technology leaders; and have common customers, problems, and opportunities.

Our brief look ahead also means that new segmentation challenges will rise to the forefront. Based on research from marketing experts, our segmentation crystal ball reveals this scenario. Static segmentation will start to be replaced by dynamic segmentation by progressive companies.[8] The former approach means that a segmentation analysis has been conducted and a basic strategy developed that may be unchanged for months or years. The latter approach uses customer behavior (e.g., purchases and preferences) to resegment markets on a regular basis.

Instead of a focus on the customer's business, superior segmenters will turn to understanding their customers' customers to do a better job of segmenting their markets.[9] This requires an in-depth exploration of the buying behavior of all of the players in the value chain—focal company, intermediaries, and final users. A more strategic view of segmentation is necessary, one that encompasses competitive advantage, market orientation, and resource allocation.[10] Finally, industrial marketers will extend segmentation decisions from simple transactions to complex buyer-seller relationships. In this latter environment, an increased strategic focus stressing an in-depth understanding of customer characteristics, current and future needs and wants, and type of business relationship desired is advisable.[11]

SUMMARY

Segmentation will continue to grow in stature as a fundamental marketing tool and foundation for marketing strategy in business organizations, large and small. While the customization movement is clearly important, in the near term, it will not replace market segmentation as a core marketing strategy—generally customers have a limited number of similar needs and wants. The two critical issues for business marketing management are (1) the adaptation and effective/efficient utilization of segmentation bases and (2) the successful implementation of segmentation findings within the firm.

Since senior executives and MBA graduates realize the value of segmentation as a precursor to developing sound marketing strategy, expect more research, training, and publications in this area. Firms in all industries (industrial, high-tech, and business service companies) are discovering the power of this strategic marketing tool for attracting and retaining customers in globally competitive markets. How about you?

PART IV:
SEGMENTATION STRATEGY CASES

Case 1

Collins Aviation Services: Building a Cluster-Based Segmentation Model

Rockwell Collins is a producer of avionics products used in a variety of military, commercial, and corporate aircraft applications. As part of a strategy to build service revenues, the firm spun off its service organization under a separate business enterprise called Collins Aviation Services (CAS). The previous service organization consisted of four distinct cost centers, one assigned to each of the firm's primary business units: Government Systems (GS), Air Transport Systems, Business and Regional Systems (BRS), and Passenger Systems (PS). The $450 million per year service unit (CAS) reports directly to the firm's CEO as a new enterprise.

A primary mission of CAS is to build value-added services from the technical and maintenance support traditionally provided at no additional charge to customers of the firm's avionics products. To grow out of this "entitlement" mode, the company embarked on a mission to invest and build alliances in pursuit of broader business solutions that would be offered on a "fee for service" basis.

MARKET DEFINITION AND SEGMENTATION

High-Level Portfolio Management

Since its inception in 1999, CAS has defined its markets along the lines of internal product support groups: Maintenance, Technical Op-

---

Case prepared by James Barry and included in this text with his permission. Mr. Barry has twenty-five years of experience in strategic planning and marketing. He has worked for Rockwell Collins, General Electric, BF Goodrich, and start-up organizations.

erations, Materials, and Aftermarket Equipment (see Exhibit 1.1). Further segmentation is provided along the lines of geography and business portfolios as a means of aligning CAS with the other enterprises (GS, BRS, PS).

The selected segmentation scheme provides a consistent planning tool for annual resource allocation planning and business performance reviews. Shown in Exhibit 1.2 are the forecasted segments the company recorded as part of its strategic financial plan. Sales are segmented by broad territories (international versus domestic), business unit affiliation, and CAS core competence portfolio. This is a rather internal view of the world and will likely impair future business growth unless a more customer-centric form of segmentation is applied.

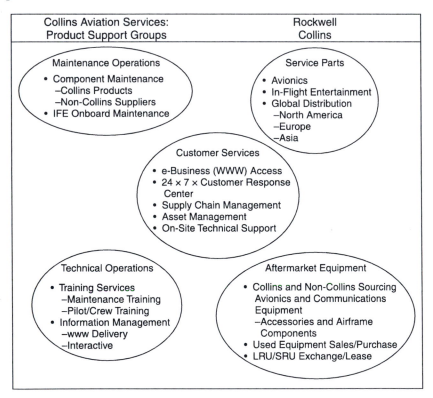

EXHIBIT 1.1. Market Segmentation by Product Support Groups

	FY01	FY02	FY03	FY04	FY05	FY06
Maintenance (MRO)						
Air Transport Systems	$48.8	$37.7	$35.8	$35.8	$37.2	$38.7
Business and Regional	$49.9	$50.0	$55.0	$57.8	$60.7	$63.7
Government Systems	$17.4	$20.5	$23.6	$27.1	$31.2	$35.9
Passenger Systems	$53.5	$50.0	$37.5	$25.0	$25.0	$27.5
Domestic MRO	$169.6	$158.2	$151.9	$145.7	$154.1	$165.8
International	$123.4	$117.0	$117.0	$128.7	$141.6	$155.8
Total Maintenance	$293.0	$275.2	$268.9	$274.4	$295.7	$321.6
Service Parts						
Air Transport Systems	$72.5	$57.1	$54.2	$54.2	$56.4	$58.7
Business and Regional	$19.8	$24.4	$24.4	$25.6	$26.9	$28.2
Government Systems	$23.8	$25.3	$29.1	$33.5	$38.5	$44.3
Passenger Systems	$27.4	$24.4	$18.3	$15.6	$16.4	$18.9
Total Service Parts	$143.5	$131.2	$126.0	$128.9	$138.2	$150.1
Technical Operations						
Air Transport Systems	$0.5	$0.2	$0.2	$0.2	$0.2	$0.2
Business and Regional	$1.7	$2.0	$4.1	$8.4	$12.6	$17.0
Government Systems	$12.3	$11.1	$22.8	$45.5	$59.5	$64.7
Passenger Systems	$0.2	$0.0	$0.0	$0.0	$0.0	$0.0
Total Technical Ops	$14.7	$13.3	$27.1	$54.1	$72.3	$81.9
Aftermarket Spares						
Air Transport Systems	$2.8	$24.7	$27.0	$29.5	$32.3	$35.4
Business and Regional	$28.6	$38.0	$40.2	$42.6	$45.1	$47.8
Government Systems	$0.0	$2.0	$2.2	$2.4	$2.6	$2.9

EXHIBIT 1.2. Sales Projections (in Millions)

An additional form of segmentation is provided at the CAS executive level to demonstrate how much business can be achieved from current clients versus new accounts (new installed base) and new service initiatives. This form of segmentation is useful to executives critical of the market share growth rationale. Finally, the company has attempted some segmentation by customer groupings (Exhibit 1.3) as further input to the executive review process. The company currently services about 3,000 customers.

Up to this point, the described segmentation includes information useful primarily to senior management and strategic planning staff in their annual planning exercises. Such information, however, has little, if any, value to sales and marketing organizations seeking direction on target prospects.

Commercial	Defense
• Airlines	• Department of Defense
• Air Freight Carriers	—Depots
• Regional Operators	Air Force
• Fractional Jet Operators	Navy
• Corporate and Business Jet Owners	Coast Guard
• Training Suppliers	Army
• Simulator Manufacturers	—Defense Logistics Agency
• Dealers	• Foreign Ministry of Defense
	• Platform OEM Primes

• Third-Party Suppliers
• Original Equipment Manufacturers
• Used Equipment Dealers

EXHIBIT 1.3. Segmentation by Customer Groups

In a move to become more sales oriented, the product-oriented enterprises were assigned service revenue goals as a means of incentivizing the sales organizations to bundle services in their product bids. The segmented information has not been well adopted, however, as sales personnel lack the opportunity characterizations required to target prospects. For example, little is known of the corporate culture, national culture, channel characteristics, or overall firmographics of top service prospects that would help sales personnel target key service accounts.

Usage Segmentation

The company is now undergoing a segmentation process that will help it qualify prospects based on channels to market. For example, the 2001 distribution of channel opportunities is analyzed by competitive type. From this information, the greatest amount of new business appears to be in the operator channel. CAS has about half of the $80 million dollar operator channel, while airline repair shops servicing other airlines account for nearly $35 million of sales potentially available to CAS. There is little market share left to be gained in the broker segment. In contrast, CAS has about a quarter of the OEM and mod center channel—this represents an approximate $15 million segment, in total.

As a marketing tool for selling services, each product salesperson is provided a database of prospects sorted by these channel types— broker, operator, OEM, mod centers, etc. Sales personnel then refer to their marketing tool kits for a description of successful strategies applied to each segment.

Geographic Segmentation

Perhaps the weakest classification dimension used by CAS relates to geographic segmentation. Despite its worldwide market presence, little is done to qualify prospects by geographic territory. The global sales force acknowledges the great disparity in cultural characteristics that would indeed influence selling strategies. This has led the author to believe that segmentation such as that offered in Hofstede's country scoring would better characterize customers by geography as well as help identify distinct strategies for building long-term loyalty.

RECOMMENDED SEGMENTATION BY LOYALTY-BASED CHARACTERISTICS

Other segmentation variables besides country culture can help the company plan sales strategies aimed at long-term customer retention. Among the variables to consider from the literature and industry interviews are the following:

1. Degree of country collectivism (relational versus individualistic)
2. Degree of corporate stability and longevity (entrepreneurial versus institutional)
3. Degree of reliance (market constrained and service critical versus low risk from switch over)
4. Degree of fraternal connection (alliance bound versus autonomous)

An example of how sales prospects can be clustered along these dimensions is shown in Exhibit 1.4. A segment profile for one particular segment, the "Relational Harmonizers," is shown in Exhibit 1.5. Note the depth of the marketing information available through this firmographic clustering approach. As its name implies, Relational Harmonizers want to be in the relationship and seek vendors/service providers that are committed to a "partnership," deliver value, and are trustworthy.

SEGMENTATION APPLIED TO DATE

Overall, as demonstrated in Exhibit 1.6, the new service organization appears to have developed a practical segmentation framework. CAS segmented its business along dimensions useful in resource allocation planning, annual performance reviews, and competency

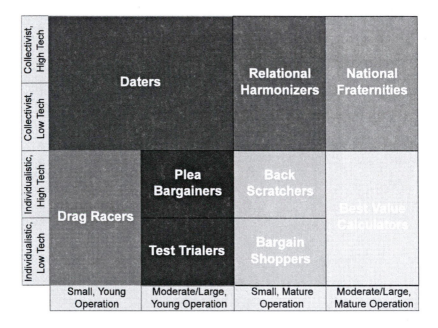

EXHIBIT 1.4. CAS's Clusters

Segment Characteristics	Behaviors	Needs
Collectivist	Governed by relational norms (solidarity, mutual goals, etc.)	Social benefits
50-100 aircraft	High emphasis on conflict resolution	High trust in supplier (benevolence)
10(+) years in business	High sense of loyalty (nonopportunistic)	Information exchange Shared values
Switching Opportunities	**Trends**	**Buyer/Supplier Power**
Incumbent performance and/or relational issues	Moderate growth	Balanced
Customers	**Competitors**	**Strategy**
Braathens	Regional brethren (other airlines)	Build social bonds (high face contact, social events)
Lan Chile	Third parties	Demonstrate benevolence, solidarity, and functional conflict resolution
Air Jamaica	OEMs	Select frontline employees in line with customer traits and values
China Eastern		Indoctrinate relational norms
Air 2000		Signal pledges (trust) with relational investments

EXHIBIT 1.5. Example Profile of the Relational Harmonizers

growth planning. From the available data, it would appear the company has more of a product/competency orientation and less of a customer-centric perspective. A recent classification of customers by channel types appears to be a good start in marrying customer channel profiles to service offerings. For future planning, a program that relates firmographic clusters to expected segment benefits and predicted relational behaviors would be most useful in sales targeting strategies as well as business forecasting.

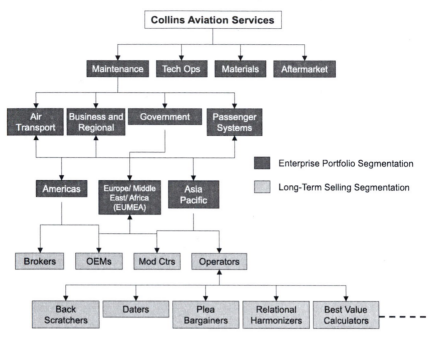

EXHIBIT 1.6. CAS's Segmentation Structure

END-OF-CASE QUESTIONS

1. Discuss the pros and cons of the CAS segmentation initiatives. Comment on distribution channels and the firmographic clustering approach.
2. Develop appropriate marketing strategies and tactics for the "Relational Harmonizers." Address the Five Ps in your response—product, price, promotion, place, and people.
3. How should CAS evolve toward customer-centric marketing?

SUGGESTED READINGS

C. Adams, "Avionics Aftermarket Services: A Buyers Market," *Avionics Magazine*, April 2002, pp. 41-45.

Geert Hofstede, "Attitudes, Values and Organizational Culture: Disentangling the Concepts," *Organization Studies,* 19(3), 1998, pp. 477-492.

Frank Jackman, "Aftermarket Networks Shaping MRO Industry," *Aviation Week and Space Technology,* 154(3), 2001, pp. 67-70.

Banwari Mittal, "Determinants of Vendor Patronage," *Journal of Business-to-Business Marketing,* 6(4), 1999, pp. 1-32.

Case 2

Dev-Soft S.A.: Segmentation and Distribution in Europe

Dev-Soft, a Spanish developer of industrial software with central offices located in Sevilla, enjoyed increasing success in Spain. The focus of Dev-Soft's business was small and medium-sized enterprises (SMEs), mainly in the agricultural and chemical industries, in need of tailor-made software solutions. During the 1990s, the competitive position of the company improved steadily, reaching an 18 percent market share in the "Industrial Computer Software and Services" sector of its domestic market.

Nevertheless, by 2002, previous market projections were not confirmed, and the demand for Dev-Soft's second product line, prepackaged software, had decreased. Market analyses showed that the sales decline was due to growing competition by large software developers. The company's core business, custom solutions, was not significantly affected by the new competition. The development of collaborative and long-term relationships with customers in need of additional or continuous support and advisory services provided Dev-Soft relative market stability. Management agreed that a shift in the competitive strategy of the firm was needed.

COMPANY BACKGROUND

Dev-Soft S.A. was founded in 1983 in the framework of the incipient Spanish software market. Felipe García, future president of the company, thought of creating a company focused on the development

Case prepared by José Manuel Ortega Egea and María Victoria Román González, PhD, of the University of Almería, Spain, and included in this text with their permission. The authors may be contacted at <jmortega@ual.es> or <mvroman@ual.es>, respectively.

of industrial software products and services adapted to the distinctive needs and characteristics of SMEs. He believed there was an opportunity for companies, having accrued the proper know-how, to develop and supply industrial software solutions to best meet the needs of SMEs.

During the 1990s, Dev-Soft had consolidated a loyal customer base, demanding not only predesigned software solutions, but also integral software support. A market study carried out in 2002 showed that the sales of prepackaged software had dropped, mainly due to increased competition by foreign enterprises in the Spanish market.

According to management, the quality and reliability of the software solutions currently developed by Dev-Soft made it possible to compete in other markets in Europe or worldwide. New possibilities enabled via Internet-related technologies increased the attractiveness of a market expansion.

Dev-Soft classified its potential customers of industrial software into two categories:

1. *Large enterprises:* These companies are characterized by greater financial resources and are able to invest more money in reliable software solutions. To a large extent, this segment purchases its software from global leaders.
2. *Small and medium-sized enterprises:* Most of the software solutions available on the market do not match the demands of SMEs because of lack of flexibility of software solutions, deficient support and advisory services after the purchase, or a poor price/quality relationship. Therefore, Dev-Soft's founders concluded that three business strategies should be emphasized:
   a. development of flexible solutions widely adapted to the customer's needs,
   b. good price/quality relationship—no trade-off between price and the quality of the products and services provided, and
   c. close contact with customers, enhanced by the geographic proximity of potential customers.

INDUSTRIAL SOFTWARE SECTOR

The Industrial Software and Services Sector includes companies involved in the design, development, marketing, and support of industrial software solutions and companies that provide computer services such as maintenance and systems integration. The services these companies provide include design automation, design analysis and optimization, computer-aided design (CAD), computer-aided engineering (CAE), and engineering software.

According to market estimations (United Nations, 2002), approximately 80 percent of the software companies offer tailor-made software services, 55 percent software packages, and 42 percent software consulting. The software sector is essentially a knowledge-based industry requiring highly skilled professionals. It is also characterized by high switching costs, because of the high costs involved in the integration of such software solutions in a company. Thus, intangible assets such as employees' know-how, customer relationships, and technology become highly relevant for software companies when developing a successful market strategy.

DEV-SOFT'S PRODUCT LINES AND PRELIMINARY DISTRIBUTION CHANNELS

The products and services offered by the company can be classified into the following categories:

- Development of tailor-made software solutions
- Prepackaged software
- Support and advisory services, including employee training, software upgrades, customer support, and other related services

These product lines require different capabilities and resources. Strong financial and marketing efforts are required to sell prepackaged software. The other product lines (adapted software solutions and support services) must emphasize the relevance of employees' know-how and customer relationships—two factors that influence service quality and customer loyalty.

The size and scope of the companies' business operations usually determine the distribution channels employed in this industry. Large software developers (approximately 67 percent market share in 2002) have their own distributors and provide their own support services, both through traditional and Internet-based channels. Smaller software developers (33 percent market share) have their own distribution centers and contracts with industrial software distributors. These companies are increasingly integrating the Internet into their distribution strategy.

The distribution channels for Dev-Soft's principal product lines are very different:

- *Prepackaged software:* The characteristics of the customer-supplier relationships for this product line are lesser cooperation, weaker bonds, lower switching costs, and less product adaptation.
- *Adapted software solutions:* The customer-supplier relationships for this product line are characterized by closer cooperation, stronger bonds, higher switching costs, and high product adaptation.

Collaboration with industrial software distributors facilitated market entry into new target areas. Nevertheless, Dev-Soft's managers agreed to progressively establish their own distribution centers in major cities in Spain. Due to the slower introduction of Internet-related technologies among Dev-Soft's customers—and Spanish enterprises, in general—the proportion of electronic B2B exchanges was relatively small for the company.

SEGMENTING THE SOFTWARE MARKET

Two driving forces induced Dev-Soft to change its business strategy and undertake a thorough market segmentation: (1) the need to respond to increased competitive pressures by foreign software developers and (2) the desire to provide better satisfaction of current customers' needs and requirements.

The company lacked previous experience carrying out formal segmentation analysis. In the past, they had taken into account only implicitly "geographic location" and "size of the companies" as segmentation criteria. Now the marketing department had to make a careful choice among a wide variety of segmentation criteria, e.g., size of the company; industry classification (SIC/NACE codes); geographic location of the company; attitudes, needs, and preferences; benefits sought by customers; etc.

The head of the marketing department stated that the segmentation should be based, ideally, on the sound identification of customer needs and wants. It was agreed that an analysis of customer needs, rather than general market trends, would provide the best segmentation results. Nevertheless, given the wider target markets the company intended to serve in the near future, other criteria were taken into account to ensure that Dev-Soft would have adequate resources to provide quality services.

Development of the Segmentation Process

To optimize the use of different segmentation dimensions, the market analysis was organized as a multistage process. The potential markets were first analyzed by firmographics. The following variables were successively included in the segmentation work: (1) customer location; (2) industry classification; (3) company size, in terms of "number of employees" and "sales volume"; and (4) customer needs-based segmentation.

Geographic Location

The markets were first segmented by location of potential customers. Although Internet-based technologies enable easier access to global markets at relatively low costs, management chose not to serve markets located too far from Spain in the early stages of international market development. Based on financial and risk considerations, the

Continental European countries, the United Kingdom, Ireland, and Russia were initial targets.

Industry

The next dimension introduced in the segmentation process was industry classification. The information about potential customers needed for this segmentation stage was obtained from a database purchased from a marketing research company. The SIC/NACE code classification was specifically used to further reduce the set of potential customers. Based on compatibility with Dev-Soft's experience, know-how, technology, and development requirements of potential customers, companies from the following industries/sectors were selected: Chemicals, Drugs, Foods and Beverages, and Manufacturing.

Size of the Company

The third "firmographic" criterion applied was the size of the company. Due to capacity, technological, and financial constraints, Dev-Soft decided to continue with its strategy of targeting SMEs from the previously identified business sectors. Two factors were used to measure the size of potential customers: number of employees and sales volume (see Exhibit 2.1). Companies with fewer than 500 employees or sales volume of less than $10 million were selected for subsequent analysis.

Customer Needs-Based Segmentation

The analysis of the potential market using firmographic criteria resulted in a set of companies scattered across different European countries. Managers within these companies were then given a market survey consisting of fourteen behavioral segmentation measures, carried out in close collaboration with an experienced international marketing research firm. Special emphasis was placed on the subjects related to support services, customer loyalty, user requirements, and current implementation and attitudes toward the Internet as a distribution channel.

SIZE OF POTENTIAL CUSTOMERS			
Number of employees	Percent	Sales volume	Percent
<100	58	< $10 million	63
100-249	9	> or equal to $10 million	37
250-499	22		
>500	11		

Exhibit 2.1. Distribution Based on Number of Employees and Sales Volume

TARGET MARKET SELECTION

In addition to development capacity, Dev-Soft employed three criteria in choosing the final set of target customers:

1. *Financial constraints:* The company was, by that time, in a healthy financial situation. Nevertheless, the strategies for the target markets were limited by the size of the company.
2. *Workforce:* The company's market expansion plans raised some questions regarding the needed skills to succeed in foreign markets, e.g., linguistic problems with foreign customers, technical preparation, and proper understanding of foreign markets.
3. *Software adaptation:* The degree of software adaptation in each market was a key consideration. The underestimation of the relevance of this factor and the costs involved with product localization could be a risk to avoid.

After a final analysis of the market research results, Dev-Soft identified target companies with the following characteristics:

- Spanish and continental European companies (including the United Kingdom, Ireland, and Russia)
- Small and medium-sized companies

- Special focus on enterprises with economic activities related to the Chemical and Agricultural Sectors
- Companies willing to use the Internet as a distribution channel
- High ratings on the relevance of "quality support services" and "loyalty in the relationship with suppliers"
- "Price" an important concern in the buying decision
- Potential customers grouped according to their needs of "product adaptation," especially taking into account linguistic criteria

REVISING THE DISTRIBUTION STRATEGY

One of the most important decisions management had to make concerned the distribution channels that would suit best the purposes of Dev-Soft in the selected markets. Should the company have its own distributors in order to keep control over the quality of the support services delivered, and the establishment of strong business bonds? Should the distribution channels be different for the various product lines and different from the ones currently used in Spain?

According to Dev-Soft's executives, the Internet should be important not only for the marketing of Dev-Soft's products and services but also for the distribution of prepackaged software in foreign markets. Market research carried out by the company showed that a high percentage of potential customers had positive attitudes toward the use of the Web for software purchases, and others had already integrated Internet-related technologies into their daily businesses.

Nevertheless, management opted not to rely solely on the Internet as a distribution channel in foreign markets. They decided to contract the services of industrial software distributors in the key market areas to assure a successful market entry.

Dev-Soft's intention is to increase the relative importance of the Internet in the distribution and marketing strategy of the company, over time. Various forecasts of B2B exchange confirm explosive growth in the next few years. According to some of them, B2B growth between 2000 and 2005 in western Europe and North America could be around 90 percent and 70 percent, respectively. Other market estimations show that worldwide B2B markets will handle $8.5 trillion by 2005. In the Spanish market it would reach $12.5 billion by 2003.

Dev-Soft's managers feel that Internet-based distribution provides great opportunities to serve extensive geographic areas with high degrees of market fragmentation. The market analyses showed that the growth of Internet-based B2B exchange would be faster in northern Europe. This situation, together with easier market access enabled by Internet-related technologies, increased considerably the attractiveness of these targeted countries.

Management perceives three additional benefits from an Internet-based B2B distribution strategy for Dev-Soft:

1. *Software development:* easier and faster market access, and faster access to information on customer requirements
2. *Marketing:* shorter delivery times, higher customer satisfaction, and valuable market information about customer needs provided by the Internet
3. *Support services:* lower costs of support services, higher satisfaction and customer loyalty

RISKS AND CHALLENGES

A number of challenges should be faced by software developers in their efforts to serve foreign markets, such as growing competition in the global markets and lack of an existing structure to support their clients in the export market.

Given the fierceness of the competitive situation, the marketing department must place strong emphasis on the continuous monitoring of customer satisfaction with Dev-Soft's software products and the delivery of quality support services.

Financial considerations must be carefully assessed too. A sound allocation of the company's limited resources is critical for its success in new markets. In addition, Dev-Soft employs highly skilled professionals with very good technical preparation. A major concern is their ability to conduct business with foreign customers. Linguistic and cultural differences between the markets are issues that management and staff will have to deal with in the near future. Although the brand status and image of the company is strong in Spain, strong international marketing efforts will be needed to establish Dev-Soft in the global marketplace.

END-OF-CASE QUESTIONS

1. Critique Dev-Soft's decision to expand overseas. Was this a wise marketing/competitive strategy?
2. How will the wider market scope impact Dev-Soft's product lines and resource allocation? What problems are likely as Dev-Soft enters new foreign markets?
3. Did the marketing department correctly organize the segmentation process? Was the selection of segmentation dimensions appropriate? What other attributes could have been used in the segmentation analyses?
4. Do you agree with the selection of distribution channels the company made based on the segmentation analysis? Given the faster growth of electronic markets in northern Europe, should Dev-Soft have relied solely on the Internet as a distribution channel for those markets?

SUGGESTED READINGS

Stavros P. Kalafatis and Markos H. Tsogas, "Business Segmentation Bases: Congruence and Perceived Effectiveness," *Journal of Segmentation in Marketing* 2(1), 1998, pp. 35-63.

Das Narayandas and Benson P. Shapiro, "SaleSoft, Inc. (A)," *Harvard Business School Case 9-596-112* (Boston: Harvard Business School Publishing, May 28, 1996).

Case 3

Dow Corning:
Segmentation and Customer Value

In 1930, Corning Glass Works began the development of a new material made from sand that combined some of the best properties of glass and plastics. Over the next decade, Corning scientists worked with the scientists at the Mellon Institute of Research in Pittsburgh to develop the promising innovation. Dow Corning was formed in 1943 as a start-up, 50/50 joint venture between Corning Glass and the Dow Chemical Company to explore and develop the commercial potential of the new technology. Over the coming decades, Dow Corning grew to be one of the most successful business joint ventures of all time, with $2.5 billion in sales and 7,500 employees worldwide.

Throughout its history, Dow Corning pioneered the development of silicon technology innovations to be used in applications as diverse as sealants and gasket-waxes and polishes, textiles and water repellent treatments, pulp and paper processing, and skin care and antiperspirants. Today, Dow Corning is the largest global producer of silicon-based materials, offering more than 7,000 different silicon-based products and services. It competes against some tremendous competitors, including GE and Bayer.

Historically, its strategy was focused on innovation and new customer applications. It focused and organized to Dominate the Segment (DTS) for customer innovation. Dow Corning grew through

Case prepared by Eric W. Balinski, Philip Allen, and J. Nicholas DeBonis. The case was extracted from their book *Value-Based Marketing for Bottom-Line Success* (New York: McGraw-Hill and the American Marketing Association, 2003), pp. 147-152, and is reprinted with permission of the McGraw-Hill Companies. Mr. Balinski may be contacted at <ebalinski@synection.net>.

discovering and delivering the most advanced technology for demanding customer applications, achieving 4,800 active patents worldwide. As such, the company was customer focused before it was fashionable to be so.

CHANGE IN THE MARKET SITUATION
FOR DOW CORNING

All market innovations inevitably mature. For a market innovator like Dow Corning, growth resulted in two businesses within one business model. In addition to business growth it achieved through innovation, Dow Corning also grew from maturing innovations that were becoming widely used in the marketplace. The latter matured to become Dow Corning's core business that loaded its sales statements and manufacturing facilities. It also attracted competition that ultimately exerted pressure on its pricing and cost position.

More insidious were the market forces that created a gap between what its maturing innovations could command in the marketplace and what had become a widespread belief in the Dow Corning culture—their commitment to customers and being "innovative" should always command a higher price. Over time, Dow Corning's business model, systems, processes, and organizational management and rewards further evolved to strengthen its innovation focus with its customers and DTS.

While Dow Corning continued to grow and innovate new products and applications with customers, the reality was that it was creating an ever larger collection of mature businesses. Paralleling its own success were customers who were innovating and growing their businesses using Dow Corning materials. Both Dow Corning and its 25,000 customers worldwide prospered together, but over time as the customers' business grew and their markets matured, the customers' value ratio or relationship changed with Dow Corning. Many customers in these maturing markets needed Dow Corning, not just to innovate new product technology, but to help them create new value through lower costs in their mature product lines to stay competitive in their markets. The need to Dominate the Cycle (DTC) of value was emerging.

For a company with a history of success through innovation, this change in customer value and needs represented a contradictory message for Dow Corning's business model. It had built a Form Follows Value* business model to effectively serve customer innovation, but the model did not serve the changing customer values that were emerging in the market. In addition, it was becoming ever clearer that some competitors who did not invest in innovating with customers were willing to buy the customers' business with a lower price.

HOW DID DOW CORNING TACKLE THIS CHALLENGE?

In the spring of 2000, Dow Corning Corporation's Electronics Industry and Advanced Engineering Materials Business Unit began to explore resegmenting its market with the intent of developing a more customer-focused strategy.

"We just knew from our customer research and from direct customer feedback that we were missing the point somewhere," recalls Ian Thackwray, the unit's general manager. "We were doing the right things in terms of getting the customer feedback and we had a mountain of knowledge in the organization, but we were struggling to know what to do with it."

The business leadership team went through an extensive strategy review, during which it realized a need to involve more people who had direct customer interface. "Our attitude had been that we didn't require needs-based segmentation in order to develop a strategy. How wrong we were," says Thackwray. "That strategy review meeting was a milestone in changing our thinking to the realization that customer needs and a true, full, and deep understanding of customer needs is fundamental to developing a meaningful and profitable business strategy."

A second meeting was convened in September 2000 with thirty-six people from the business team, technical, marketing, sales, supply

---

*Form Follows Value is a trademark of Eric W. Balinski and SYNECTION.

chain, and new business groups. The objective was to reevaluate implications of customer value segmentation as a basis for reviewing the business's strategy.

"The really exciting thing was that no one had a preconceived idea of what the outcome would be and everyone went in with an open mind," remembers Babette Pettersen, then responsible for Marketing and New Business Development in the Electronics Industry Sector. "The idea was to stimulate an open-minded reappraisal of our customer value segmentation, formulating our intimate customer knowledge alongside frameworks and segmentation approaches from both theoretical models and practical examples." The resulting set of customer value commitments was simple, but Dow Corning's Electronics Business had never developed its strategy from this customer needs-based perspective before.

"We defined and profiled each segment and we assigned customer applications into each segment, enabling us to quantify and evaluate each segment in terms of attractiveness and our ability to compete as a basis for targeting," Thackwray explains.

Based on the success of applying the value-based marketing principles in the Electronics Industry Business, similar sessions were conducted by each of the global business units. "This is where the real insight came," relates Scott Fuson, Global Executive Director Marketing and Sales. "After applying the customer needs-based segmentation methodology, we began to realize that there was a significant amount of existing customers who buy for very different reasons. This led us to develop an enterprise-wide look at our customers, then creating distinct and compelling value propositions and business models for each of the customer needs-based segments we identified.

"We were particularly excited about how this also better took advantage of our market-based structure and operations," continues Fuson. "These new business models resulted from converting the needs-based segmentation into customer-focused value that better aligned our resources and structure to improve business model performance with our customers." Dow Corning recognized that there was other real value that its customers sought.

"A critical outcome of the reevaluation is that it forced us to reappraise our entire market positioning and brand presence," Fuson explains. This included the essence, attributes, and hierarchy for the Dow Corning brand itself and the creation of an entirely new business model for customers that required a price-reliable supply. This new brand positioning became the company's XIAMETER brand.

VALUE-BASED MARKETING AT DOW CORNING: DISCOVERING AND UNDERSTANDING THE CUSTOMER

As a company built on developing customer innovation, Dow Corning had a substantial amount of customer information from numerous sources: purchased studies of its customer base, regular customer satisfaction studies conducted by an outside research firm, and regular customer feedback through its Customer Relationship Management (CRM) process.

All of this contributed to a full and deep understanding of its customers' needs and value expectations. Yet it was when Dow Corning started to look at its information from both a segmentation and a customer value perspective that the information started to tell the company new things. For example, three broad customer value segments were identified: (1) customers who innovate into new markets, (2) customers who were in fast-growing markets, and (3) customers looking to reduce costs and improve productivity in large, highly competitive markets.

Innovation-focused customers are defined as those committed to being first to the market with new technologies and state-of-the-art products, and who seek advanced innovation and creation of unique technical or market positions. Dow Corning's customer value commitment for this group of customers is both innovative solutions based on cutting-edge technologies and services and expertise in assisting customers to get their products to market faster with better value differentiators for the customers' customers.

For example, Dow Corning helped Reliance Industries reformulate its fiber-optic cable conduit inner lining to improve the lining's slipperiness. The superior slipperiness allowed fiber optics to go into conduit faster and at longer lengths. This enabled Reliance Industries' customers to install fiber-optic cables significantly faster and for 30 to 50 percent lower cost. In another instance, Dow Corning helped a consumer products company get the new household cleaner to market faster by taking on the manufacturing of the cleaner in its own facilities.

Customers in fast-growing markets are defined as those looking for easy, drop-in solutions that give them speed, efficiency, convenience, and reliability to meet growth demands. Their value drivers are lower cost offerings with proven performance and demonstrated use. For them, Dow Corning's customer value commitment offers proven performance in technology, manufacturing, and supply chain management.

Dow Corning helped a customer's global sealants and adhesives business by working with its larger customers to convert to bulk delivery systems. The change from 55-gallon drums to a new 8,000-gallon storage facility reduced handling and labor costs, dropped waste 7 percent, and freed up 10,000 square feet of space in the customer's operation.

Customers in large, highly competitive markets, typically with products in the mature stage of the product life cycle, form the third segment. These customers expect improved process efficiency and effectiveness in manufacturing to help them achieve maximum profit by reducing costs. They are looking for such things as ideas from suppliers, outsourcing capabilities, inventory control and supply chain services, and disposal assistance. Dow Corning's cost-effective solutions that drive overall costs down is the customer value commitment for this customer value segment.

One tool Dow Corning developed for these customers was software that could more precisely pinpoint lubrication for critical plant equipment. The Integrated Oil Analysis software enabled plant operations to perform a complete oil and lubrication analysis on vital equipment to optimize maintenance programs rather than follow routine scheduled maintenance.

As Thackwray makes clear, "We could define and profile each segment and we could identify customers in each segment, enabling us to quantify and evaluate each segment in terms of attractiveness and our ability to deliver a superior value to these customers." Building upon the three broad segment groupings, the electronics business identifed seven new customer value segments based on the needs and values of its customers.

The key was to take all the various inputs about customers from multiple sources and to integrate them in an interactive and creative thinking process to deliver an insightful output that helped the business better understand what really mattered to its customers' success. Dow Corning developed a summary matrix of customer value for its business. Exhibit 3.1 presents a generic segmentation framework that can be adapted by other businesses to assess customer value segments.

END-OF-CASE QUESTIONS

1. Critique Dow Corning's segmentation planning process and the resulting three broad customer value segment groupings.
2. Which target market(s) should Dow Corning pursue and why?
3. Compare and contrast Dow Corning's market targets with the four customer value segment profiles in Exhibit 3.1.
4. Which of the four customer value segments in Exhibit 3.1 (innovators, optimizers, operationalizers, and/or economizers) most resembles the target markets that your company is trying to attract or retain?
5. How can your company apply customer value thinking to improve your market segmentation analyses and strategies?

SUGGESTED READINGS

J. Nicholas Debonis, Eric W. Balinski, and Philip Allen, *Value-Based Marketing for Bottom Line Success: 5 Steps to Creating Customer Value* (New York: McGraw-Hill and The American Marketing Association, 2003).

Dow Corning Web site, <http://www.dowcorning.com/content/announce/xiameter _backgrounder.asp>.

	Segment 1: Innovators	Segment 2: Optimizers	Segment 3: Operationalizers	Segment 4: Economizers
Behavior of Customers in Segments	First to market, risk takers; reputation for the latest ideas	Fast followers; let someone else prove, then exploit market	Best at optimizing total acquisition and use costs	Focused on best pricing; trade-offs to drive cost out
Value Need in Segment	Leading ideas or technology to create edge	Fast and responsive support to make transitions	Supply chain optimization support	Continually drive costs out of business
Typical Customer Cost Drivers	R&D; marketing; engineering	Marketing; production; purchasing	Supply chain; production	Production; logistics
Customer's Profit Model	Profit generated through a stream of innovation	Profit generated by quickly capitalizing on opportunities	Efficiency of operations drives profit	Selling as much stuff as cheaply as possible drives profit
What Do These Customers Measure?	Time to market; market response; development costs	Market share and its growth; price/cost variances	Share protection; purchasing costs; supply chain costs	Purchasing costs; market share; operation costs
Customer's Market Drivers/Situation	Unique ideas are valued in market; few competitors can match	Customer sees opportunity and battles over growth in market	Market is mature; need to win the race to run efficiently	Market declining but these customers hang on
Leading Competitive Offering/ Situation	Competitor wants to play one-upmanship	Variable offerings with high differentiation to attract customers	Unbundling of offerings and à la carte purchasing	Suppliers are exiting, but some will streamline operations to survive
Your Strategic Value Commitment	Centered on driving innovation in ideas, products, and solutions	Centered on helping customers capture growth opportunities	Centered on streamlining supply chain, ease of doing business	Centered on driving every possible cost out

EXHIBIT 3.1. Generic Customer Value Segment Matrix

Case 4

Lexmark International: Creating New Market Space

Creating new market space is an approach that forward-thinking companies can use to achieve a competitive marketing advantage. This case addresses the six components of new market space (substitute industries, strategic groups within an industry, redefining buyer groups, complementary products and services, functional and emotional industry orientation, and time), individually and collectively. We will explain how Lexmark International utilized (and might have utilized) several of these strategic differentiators as it went head-to-head with the leading manufacturers in the global printer industry.

INTRODUCTION

A cohesive strategy is essential for understanding and improving a company's business performance. This strategy should include a clear approach that is designed to outthink and outvalue rivals. Many companies are overwhelmed by fierce competition. Some companies lack the ability to recognize and adjust to trends. Others are unable to acquire and exploit market intelligence that is readily available. Others simply do not have the wherewithal to stay in the market, let alone leapfrog the competition.

Case prepared by Jude Edwards, DIBA, and Art Weinstein, PhD. Dr. Edwards is a Market Analyst at Lockheed Martin, Aircraft Traffic Management, and an Adjunct Professor in the Graduate School, Capitol College of Engineering, Laurel, Maryland. An earlier version of this case was published in Brenda Ponsford (ed.), *Proceedings of the Association of Marketing Theory and Practice Annual Meeting* (Hilton Head, SC: Association of Marketing Theory and Practice, March 27-29, 2003), pp. 2.3: 5-9.

Rather than focusing on building market share, market-driving firms such as Amazon.com, CNN, Dell, FedEx, and SAP have revolutionized their industries. These innovative companies have created new markets or redefined their businesses to make competitors inferior or obsolete.

Creating new market space (hereafter abbreviated as NMS) is a marketing response and strategic model for extending growth in maturing or matured markets. This may be best understood from the perspective that specific markets are already saturated with products and suppliers, yet creative entrepreneurial companies can redesign the competitive landscape by redefining markets to find new business opportunities.

This case study examines the components associated with NMS as a fresh approach to market definition/segmentation strategy. The Lexmark International case demonstrates how NMS ideas can be employed to gain a competitive advantage in the printer industry. Finally, this case concludes by offering guidelines for marketing professionals and managers on how to compete in new market arenas.

WHAT IS NEW MARKET SPACE?

Kim and Mauborgne (1999) state that innovation is the only way that companies can break free from the pack when faced with cutthroat competition. It is essential that organizations stake out a fundamentally new market space by creating products or services for which there are no direct competitors. This suggests that the best companies have developed processes and/or strategies for "cornering the market" or "nailing down" particular market niches.

Defining markets is not a one-shot effort; rather, it requires fine-tuning and periodic reviews. Guidelines for defining market spaces were provided by Vandermerwe (2000):

1. Take an integrated view of the customer.
2. Look for arenas that are greater than the sum of the core items.
3. Find market spaces that can be expanded over time.

4. Bridge product lines.
5. Cut across industry boundaries.
6. Span customer activities over a lifetime.

As Kim and Mauborgne (1999) explain, creating NMS consists of six areas of comparative opportunity for managers to evaluate in making effective market decisions (see Exhibit 4.1). This approach can work well for both early entrants and latecomers in the marketplace. Note that Lexmark International was a late entrant into the global printer industry. The next section details how Lexmark employed NMS initiatives in its market planning.

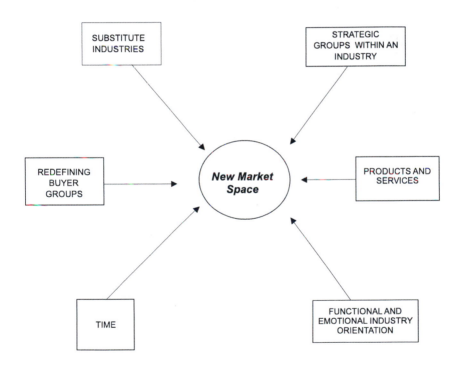

EXHIBIT 4.1. The Six Parameters of New Market Space (*Source:* Adapted from Chan W. Kim and Renee Mauborgne, "Creating New Market Space," *Harvard Business Review*, 77[1], 1999, pp. 129-142.)

LEXMARK INTERNATIONAL:
NMS AS A COMPETITIVE MARKETING TOOL

Lexmark International is a twelve-year-old company that began as an IBM spin-off. The company develops and owns innovative technologies that have won more than 800 awards from technology and business publications worldwide. Lexmark has grown to become a global leader in printing solutions (printers, supplies, and services). In the year 2000, the company generated more than $3.8 billion in revenue, earned a half a billion dollars in profit, and obtained 56 percent of its business from international markets.

Clearly, a key ingredient in the Lexmark success formula was its ability to apply ideas that reside in the domain of NMS. Were these NMS principles executed in a deliberate way, i.e., as part of Lexmark's global strategy? It is difficult to know the answer to this query, for sure. It is interesting and worthwhile, however, to examine how several of these elements became part of Lexmark's global marketing strategy.

The first element associated with creating NMS is the concept of "looking across substitute industries." As an extreme example, one might argue that postage stamps, e-mail service, long-distance telephone calls, video conferencing, and airline tickets are all competitive offerings. To achieve and sustain an effective presence in global markets, it is necessary to design and execute an integrated strategy that covers the full spectrum of market entries across a variety of industries.

Undoubtedly, Lexmark employed this strategy by using its typewriter products and industry contacts to pave the way for its dot-matrix and low-end laser printers. With the market well established for these products, Lexmark then moved on to the next stage of its overall strategy—tapping market segments for its top-of-the-line laser printers. From the outset, it appears that Lexmark intentionally used a substitute industry (typewriters) to develop a viable market for its emerging high-end laser printer sector. Early generation Lexmark products such as typewriters and dot-matrix printers provided brand recognition, price leadership, and quality signaling to the marketplace; this yielded a competitive advantage over less diversified mass and niche market players in the global printing industry.

Second, Lexmark created NMS by targeting "strategic groups within each industry." Strategic groups are companies within an industry that pursue a similar strategy, often based on price and performance dimensions. Initially, the company's market included users of laser printers, dot-matrix printers, and typewriters. Lexmark competed in a strategic group that targeted end users who did not have an immediate need for high-end laser printing (the firm created a new market segment in the industry). These customers were located in many different industries and came from various geographical areas around the world.

Lexmark divided the international market into three regions in scanning the global market horizon: (1) the United States; (2) Canada, Latin America, and Asia Pacific; and (3) Europe, the Middle East, and Africa. In emerging markets, prospects often lacked the purchasing power to buy expensive equipment and the necessary training to maximize the printing power of advanced technologies. Since many developing countries lacked the technological infrastructure to absorb its laser and color inkjet printers, Lexmark formulated a strategy to capture the typewriter and dot-matrix business; later, it introduced more sophisticated printers as the economies of each country allowed. Hence, Lexmark targeted these buyers as long-term (lifelong) strategic customers.

Third, Lexmark achieved a competitive advantage by "redefining buyer groups." It exploited information by collecting market intelligence about end users. As Porter's (1986) value chain theory suggests, the bargaining/purchasing power of the buyer is a fundamental market consideration. Lexmark clearly recognized the importance of buyers. As an example, the company provided low-end, but high-quality laser printers to specific customers whose needs were not met by Hewlett-Packard. (*Note:* HP laser printers were often priced beyond the purchasing power of average consumers.) Since its inception into the printer market, it was Lexmark's strategy to introduce a variety of laser printers to meet market needs that were previously untapped by the competition. As a result, Lexmark outperformed Hewlett-Packard and other rivals in many key segments of the laser printer market.

Fourth, it can be shown that Lexmark obtained a competitive advantage, particularly for it high-end laser products, by offering "complementary products and services" to its typewriter and dot-matrix customers. Lexmark developed channel relationships by providing quality goods and services that met immediate customer needs. Strategic alliances were created with local distributors in host countries that allowed the distributors the freedom to design their own effective marketing strategies and programs. Lexmark also provided training to enable intermediaries and customers to better utilize its products. Later, the company rolled out upgraded products and services for the international markets, as needed. Thus, Lexmark created NMS by providing complementary products and service where the competition failed to do so, and Lexmark achieved a global competitive advantage in the process.

In considering Lexmark's overall marketing strategy and performance, a fifth point can be stated: the company achieved a competitive advantage over "time." The company's objective is to develop and keep customers for life. Initially, Lexmark acquired new business by meeting customers' basic printing needs, using dot-matrix printers, other low-end printer types, or services. Many of these customers were located in developing regions of the world with limited funds or capacity to absorb high-end laser products. Over time, as these countries, companies, and customers expanded their capacity and economic and technical infrastructures, Lexmark introduced state-of-the-art laser printers into those markets. A variety of other customer-specific services and products were also provided. This strategic planning process was fine-tuned with the introduction of each new version/product into designated market segments.

In sum, five approaches for creating new market space were effectively utilized by Lexmark International, a late market entrant, to forge a competitive marketing advantage in the global printer industry. (*Note:* we did not find sufficient information to comment on the functional and emotional orientation of the industry.) When existing domestic or international markets are saturated with competitors and their associated products, NMS techniques may provide the needed competitive edge to win customers and build market share. Lexmark's business performance relative to the five NMS elements discussed is summarized in Exhibit 4.2.

LEXMARK AND NEW MARKET SPACE: SOME LESSONS LEARNED .

How can NMS concepts be used as a strategic business tool by managers and marketing professionals to gain a competitive advantage in international markets? As a starting point, the marketing strategy should enhance the business performance. Consider Lexmark's global expansion into new regions. For example, Lexmark recently entered the subcontinent of India through a joint venture with a local Indian partner. It will be noteworthy to observe Lexmark's performance in the world's second largest country over the next few years. Hence, multiple business strategies (some NMS based and others not NMS based) need to be executed in different parts of the world to achieve marketing advantages.

NMS Dimensions	Lexmark's Strategy	Lexmark's Performance
Substitute industries	Typewriters	4—Successful
Strategic groups	Matched corporate printer line to country-specific needs	4—Successful
Buyer groups	Low-end, quality laser printers	3—Somewhat successful
Complementary products and services	High-end laser printers; training and services	5—Very successful
Time	Develop and keep customers for life	5—Very successful

EXHIBIT 4.2. How Lexmark Captured New Market Space

In addition, the proposed NMS concepts are useful as a complementary competitive tool to strategies that are currently being used by companies in any market. While it is not necessary that all six components of creating NMS be utilized, the right combination may prove sufficiently effective in penetrating and expanding a market base. Five additional implications of creating NMS are suggested:

1. NMS advocates that a company extend its competitive reach by looking across substitute industries. In contrast, niche marketing narrows an organization's scope by focusing on a single segment of a market.
2. Strategic groups within industries or markets can be cultivated to build new competitive alliances.
3. Creating NMS recognizes and effectively manages the trade-offs between the bargaining power of buyers and end users.
4. A product development culture is nurtured. This competitive strategy extends product life cycles and fosters relevant new product and service offerings.
5. The concept of time is based on building long-term relationships and creating customers for life. The different ways in which various cultures deal with the idea of time must be carefully assessed.

FUTURE PROSPECTS

Finally, the recent Dell-Lexmark alliance, whereby Lexmark will manufacture low-end, Dell-branded inkjet and laser printers and supplies, which threatens Hewlett-Packard's market leadership, is worthy of careful analysis. As of 2002, HP had about a 43 percent share of the world's printer market, followed by Epson (22 percent) and Lexmark (14 percent). The Dell-Lexmark team, led by Dell's PC marketing muscle, may alter this competitive landscape considerably. An in-depth study of relevant NMS concepts in this context may be enlightening.

END-OF-CASE QUESTIONS

1. How can your company apply the ideas of creating NMS?
2. What impact does the size of the company have on using these guidelines?
3. Compare and contrast NMS concepts to niche marketing and market segmentation?
4. What changes would be called for if Lexmark International applied NMS thinking to the European Union, Japan, or Latin America?
5. Critique the Dell-Lexmark joint venture from a segmentation and market space perspective.

SUGGESTED READINGS

Chan W. Kim and Renee Mauborgne, "Creating New Market Space," *Harvard Business Review*, 77(1), 1999, pp. 83–93.

Nirmalya Kumar, Lisa Scheer, and Philip Kotler, "From Market Driven to Market Driving," *European Management Journal*, 18(2), 2000, pp. 129-142.

Lexmark International Annual Report (Lexington, KY: Lexmark, 2001).

B. Pimentel,"Dell Computer Signs Printer Deal with Lexmark," *San Francisco Chronicle*, September 25, 2002, online edition.

Michael E. Porter, *Competition in Global Industries* (Boston: Harvard Business School Press, 1986).

Franklin R. Root, *Entry Strategies for International Markets* (San Francisco: Lexington Books, 1994).

Sandra Vandermerwe, "How Increasing Value to Customers Improves Business Results," *Sloan Management Review*, Fall 2000, pp. 27-37.

Art Weinstein, "Market Redefinition: Strategies and Guidelines for Technology Executives," *Competitive Intelligence Review*, 6(3), 1995, pp. 52-57.

Art Weinstein, *Defining Your Market: Winning Strategies for High-Tech, Industrial, and Service Firms* (Binghamton, NY: The Haworth Press, 1998).

Case 5

Pharmacia Corporation: Pharmaceutical Segmentation

INDUSTRY OVERVIEW

Pharmacia is one of the top pharmaceutical companies in the world. The recent merger with industry leader Pfizer increased its global market share from 4 to 12 percent. (GlaxoSmithKline, the second major player in the industry, has slightly more than 7 percent global share.) Pfizer and Pharmacia will bring 11 one-billion-dollar products (in revenues) to the pipeline and approximately fifteen new products within the next five years.

BRIEF HISTORY

Pharmacia traces its roots back to 1853 when a leading Italian pharmacist started his own company. In 1931 the company merged with Kabi Pharmacia. In 1995 Pharmacia merged with Upjohn, an established Michigan company. In 2000, Monsanto, Pharmacia, and Upjohn completed a merger, creating a dynamic new competitor in the industry, Pharmacia Corporation.

In 2002, Pfizer acquired Pharmacia Corporation, making it the largest pharmaceutical company in the world. Sales for Pharmacia alone exceeded $13 billion in 2001. There are six key pharmaceutical products: Celebrex (arthritis/inflammation), Bextra (arthritis and dysmenor-

Case prepared by Carolyn Saenz, a sales consultant for Pharmacia Corporation. Input provided by Mr. Taeho Oh, Managed Care Director for the Southeast Region, and other Pharmacia team members/management. Ms. Saenz may be contacted at <carolyn@ carolynsaenz.com>.

rhea), Xalatan (open-angle glaucoma), Detrol (overactive bladder), Camptosar (colorectal cancer), and Zyvox (gram-positive infections). The company's major markets are the United States, Japan, Argentina, Italy, Brazil, Canada, France, United Kingdom, Germany, and Mexico.

INDUSTRY CHALLENGES AND MARKET SEGMENTATION

A new conservatism within the world's most important regulatory agency, the U.S. Food and Drug Administration (FDA), is slowing product flow within the industry and introducing many uncertainties. Delays in new product flow are adding stress to those companies that are losing marketed products to generic erosion. In addition, reduced government revenues are increasing pressure for tighter health care budgets and more stringent price controls on drugs. One of the greatest challenges is to build new and better medicines, providing patients and physicians with a choice of the best and newest treatments. In order to accomplish this, companies must implement strategic segmentation plans for physicians, patients, and managed care organizations. Exhibits 5.1 through 5.3 show how Pharmacia practices segmentation at the corporate, division, and sales rep levels.

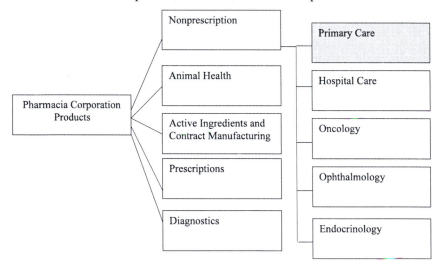

EXHIBIT 5.1. Company's Product Segmentation

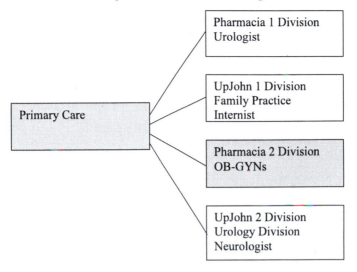

EXHIBIT 5.2. Sales Division Segmentation—Primary Care

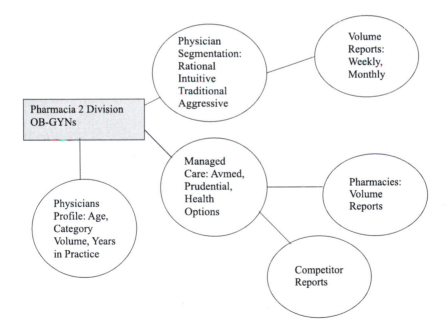

EXHIBIT 5.3. Sales Representative Segmentation Tools

PHARMACEUTICAL SEGMENTATION BASES

The pharmaceutical industry is in need of more segmentation tools in an ongoing effort to establish close and sustainable relationships with customers. Market segmentation is the method of choice for identifying and influencing target groups. A predominant approach in this industry is to crudely divide physicians into categories such as rational, intuitive, traditional, or aggressive. Some companies segment customers as "dynamic innovators" or "old conservatives." Other segmentation approaches used in the pharmaceutical industry include these:

1. *Heavy versus light users:* Prior to 1996, Pharmacia operated on the basis of key heavy users or prescription volume to segment the market; for example, a physician's volume was the predictor for the product potential. Today, physicians are segmented into heavy versus light users or loyal versus nonloyal customers.

2. *Buying styles segmentation:* There are four basic buying styles:

   a. *Control and choice:* These physicians are drivers and tend to be directive, to the point, and fast moving. They are categorized as outgoing and task oriented, focused on the bottom line. These physicians like a challenge, so appeal to their sense of individual accomplishment.

   b. *Attention and approval:* These physicians are spontaneous and people oriented. Physician who exhibit this style want to connect with their patients. They tend to be more expressive and want to inspire and influence others. These physicians buy because they will stand out from the crowd and their sense of popularity and position will be fulfilled.

   c. *Quality and correctness:* These physicians have a need for facts and figures to determine product quality and perceived correctness. They are logical and analytical and tend to be cautious. These customers buy as a result of the representatives' accuracy and accountability.

   d. *Safety and security:* These physicians are steady and supportive. Physicians who exhibit this style want things to be the same and they know what they like. Representatives should emphasize the safety and efficacy information of the drugs.

3. *Demographics:* Constant demographic changes will continue to provide the industry with opportunities for growth well into the future. People are living longer and enjoying active lifestyles at an older age; they are demanding new and better medicines to help them maintain their quality of life. Even with the dramatic advances in science in recent years, there is a wide range of unmet medical needs in disease areas as cancer, inflammation, stroke, Alzheimer's, depression, and asthma. Pharmacia Corporation has taken advantage of this opportunity and has launched different medicines to cover these areas. For example, the launch of the hormone replacement drug Activella in 1998 opened a window for better health and management of symptoms for menopausal patients. Detrol, introduced in 1998, allows patients to have more bladder control and increased quality of life.

4. *Managed care segmentation:* Managed care influences physicians' prescription behavior. Physicians are segmented by managed care plan activity and patient volume within each plan. Short-term promotional campaigns are implemented to advise physicians of formulary changes, especially if a medication is the first choice in a particular plan.

5. *Segment based on region:* Each sales representative is responsible for a group of zip codes or regions. Some regions, such as New York City, Chicago, or Miami, have a large volume of prescriptions within a small region in contrast to Ohio or Tennessee where physician offices tend to be distant from one another. These regions are segmented into business volume for each zip code. The representative manages the territory according to prescription volume, managed care trends, and individual business potential.

AN RX FOR PHARMACEUTICAL SEGMENTATION

We are entering an age of increasingly individualized or segmented health care. Pharmaceutical companies have to start dealing with smaller customer groups. This case deals with different aspects of the pharmaceutical segmentation; however, there is not a universal direction for segmenting customers. This industry must analyze customers (physicians and patients) by factors such as demographics and specialties and identify precise targets. There is a need for microsegmentation, a far more individualized approach to doing business. The suggested approach includes these steps:

1. Segment groups on the basis of health behavior, not physician specialty.
2. Develop the best offering for segments in terms of content, interactive tools, marketing messages, and information for consumers and physicians.
3. Segment by diverse patient populations and languages.
4. Segment into narrow therapeutic indications.
5. Develop a comprehensive model to predict physicians' prescribing behavior based on multiple, relevant segmentation variables.

END-OF-CASE QUESTIONS

1. Critique Pharmacia's approach to segmenting markets.
2. How can Pharmacia improve its physician segmentation plan? Consider prescription sales potential, regional markets, account-specific information, product differentiation, and behavioral approaches in your analysis.
3. What variables should be part of an integrated pharmaceutical segmentation model?

SUGGESTED READINGS

Richard C. Anderson, "Promotional Planning Without the Guesswork: ROI Analyses Lead the Way," *Pharmaceutical Executive,* February 2002.

Best Practices, LLC. "Benchmarking Reports Summary: Targeting Pharmaceutical Customers Through Market Segmentation," SM-128.

Graham Hurrell et al., "Solpadol—A Successful Case of Brand Positioning," *Journal of Market Research Society,* July 1997, p. 463.

Christopher Kuenne, "Segment-Based Marketing: Part 2," *Pharmaceutical Executive,* October 2000.

Christopher Kuenne and Lawrence Choi, "Segment-Based Marketing: From Dream to Reality," *Pharmaceutical Executive,* October 2000, pp. 54-68.

Dan Saren and Howard Marmorstein, "Identifying New Patient Prospects: Efficacy on Usage Segmentation," *Journal of Health Care Marketing,* Spring 1996.

Case 6

Sportmed: Market Definition and Benefit Segmentation

Sportmed, a $100 million company, sells medical instruments and supplies to physicians who practice sports medicine—the treatment of sports-related injuries. This case illustrates how the company applies creative market definition and segmentation to maximize customer and shareholder value and reinvent itself in a changing marketplace.

SPORTMED'S CUSTOMERS

Sportmed set the boundaries of its sports medicine instruments business area to be global in scope in order to encompass its customer base and its competitive threats. The customers for sports medicine instruments seek to satisfy the product needs of advanced features, multiple functions (the instruments can test for several injury or disease conditions), accuracy, and ease of use. Customers also seek to satisfy the nonproduct needs of ongoing education, service, reassurance through the company's image and reputation, and information provided through consultative selling.

Sportmed is a real but disguised company. This case was originally prepared by Alan S. Cleland and Albert V. Bruno. It was extracted from their book *The Market Value Process: Bridging Customer and Shareholder Value* (San Francisco: Jossey-Bass Publishers, 1996). The scoring approach to market definition described in the case is part of the Market Value Process. For further information, contact Mr. Cleland at Cleland and Associates, Palo Alto, California. This case has been reprinted with permission and adapted by Art Weinstein, PhD. An abbreviated version of this case appeared in Dr. Weinstein's book *Defining Your Market: Winning Strategies for High-Tech, Industrial, and Service Firms* (Binghamton, NY: The Haworth Press, 1998).

Sportmed felt that all customers had the same broad set of four product needs and four nonproduct needs; however, the importance they attribute to those needs areas differs. For example, a young sports medicine physician may be just out of medical school and setting up her practice. She may be price sensitive because she has limited resources to invest. Due to her medical training, she may place great importance on advanced features and may value information provided via consultative selling. In contrast, an older sports medicine practitioner may be less price sensitive because he is well established in his field. He may be content with the current product offerings and see little advantage in the latest technology. Since his education is less current, he may value information updates through sales calls or ongoing educational programs.

SPORTMED'S MARKET DEFINITION

Markets can be defined based on customer groups (whose price, product, and nonproduct needs are being met), customer needs (what price, product, and nonproduct needs are being met), and technologies (how price, product, and nonproduct needs are being met). Customer groups are defined by age (young and older practitioners) and specialty (sports medicine specialists [SMS] and general practitioners [GP]). Customer needs are defined by benefits (progressives and traditionals) and patient diagnosis (muscle and tendon and other). Technology is defined in terms of technologies for delivering results (computer display or printout) and the testing technologies employed (nonmicroprocessor based versus microprocessor based).

While this discussion has been limited to two approaches in each category, there is no set limit to the number of approaches an organization should consider using to define its market most effectively. Sportmed's management ultimately felt that the specialty (customer groups), benefits (customer needs), and testing technology (technology) approaches were the most promising choices for the three identified market definition dimensions. As Exhibit 6.1 shows, each Sportmed customer and potential customer can be assigned to one of eight potential market segments.

1. Sports Medicine Practitioners/Progressives/Nonmicroprocessors
2. Sports Medicine Practitioners/Progressives/Microprocessors
3. Sports Medicine Practitioners/Traditionals/Nonmicroprocessors
4. Sports Medicine Practitioners/Traditionals/Microprocessors
5. General Practitioners/Progressives/Nonmicroprocessors
6. General Practitioners/Progressives/Microprocessors
7. General Practitioners/Traditionals/Nonmicroprocessors
8. General Practitioners/Traditionals/Microprocessors

EXHIBIT 6.1. The Initial Eight Sportmed Segments

EXTENDING THE MARKET DEFINITION ANALYSIS

Sportmed assigned all potential customers (its own and the competitors') into medical specialty and benefit segments. Sports medicine specialists attached more importance to quality (product and nonproduct) than to price.

Generalists, however, were considerably more price sensitive. Progressives were early adopters of new technology and willing to "pay up" for the competitive edge this equipment gave them in their medical practice. Traditionals were more cautious customers who waited to adopt new technology until it had been broadly accepted in the market; they were willing to forego possible competitive advantage in their medical practice and believe in "playing it safe."

A summary of the various weights by market segment and customer buying decision factors is provided in Exhibit 6.2. While both specialty and benefits are useful discriminators of purchase likelihood, the benefits approach is somewhat better based on total D-scores (60 versus 40).

Based on this analysis, Sportmed chose benefits as the approach it would focus on in its initial market definition. (*Note:* management plans on repeating this process annually.) Furthermore, progressives would be offered a line of high-end instruments reflecting the reality that quality factors accounted for nearly two-thirds of the buying decision. In contrast, traditionals would be targeted with a line of low-

	SMS	GP	D-Score	PROG	TRAD	D-Score
Price	40	60	20	35	65	30
Product	30	26	4	32.5	21	11.5
Nonproduct	30	14	16	32.5	14	18.5
Total D-Score	N/A	N/A	40	N/A	N/A	60

EXHIBIT 6.2. Customer Buying Decision Assessments (SMS = sports medicine specialists; GP = generalists; PROG = progressives; TRAD = traditionals; D-Score = differences by specialty or benefits)

end instruments, since price is the critical buying motivator (accounting for 65 percent of the decision). Sportmed realized that whatever modest attention it gave to quality in the low-end market should emphasize product needs rather than nonproduct needs. Exhibit 6.3 reviews the characteristics of Sportmed's two benefit segments.

STRATEGIC MARKETING CONSIDERATIONS

This simple but powerful first cut at a precision strategy for each market amply rewarded the effort Sportmed had invested in creative market definition by winning new customers. Sportmed's thirty-person top management group, including the president, divided itself into planning teams to build integrated customer value strategies in each of the markets it defined.

As an example, Sportmed devised the message "Leading-edge software boosts diagnostic precision" as the foundation for its media campaign. This message nicely communicates features, accuracy, education, and consultative selling—important buying motivators to progressive practitioners. Ads in sports medicine journals, direct mail to prescription-writing physicians, and a trade show booth at a national sports medicine convention represented the heart of the promotional campaign.

	Traditionals	Progressives
Benefit (primary)	Good price	Quality and value (products, services, and price)
Buying motive	"Play it safe"	"Leading-edge technology"
Market opportunities	Core market, international	Emerging market—high perceived value of new technologies
Price/product	Low-end instruments	High-end instruments
Product life cycle	Mature markets in United States, growth abroad	Growth stage—early adopters
User type	GP, SMS	SMS

EXHIBIT 6.3. Sportmed's Proposed Benefit Segments

END-OF-CASE QUESTIONS

1. Critique the market definition/segmentation approach used by Sportmed. What improvements would you suggest to management?
2. Would you advise Sportmed to concentrate its marketing on the progressives? Why or why not?
3. Should other factors besides price and quality be evaluated for the market segments?
4. What impact would cost factors, competition, perceived value, and market share likely have on Sportsmed's market analysis and marketing strategy?

SUGGESTED READINGS

Alan S. Cleland and Albert V. Bruno, *The Market Value Process: Bridging Customer and Shareholder Value* (San Francisco: Jossey-Bass Publishers, 1996).
Art Weinstein, *Defining Your Market: Winning Strategies for High-Tech, Industrial, and Service Firms* (Binghamton, NY: The Haworth Press, 1998).

Notes

Preface

1. Allen C. Stines, *B-to-B Market Management Competencies: An Emergent Model,* 2003. Allen can be contacted at <allen.stines@b2bcompetencies.com> or (800) 804-7503.

2. Donald R. Lehmann, "What's on Marketers' Minds?" *Marketing Services Directory* (Chicago: American Marketing Association, 2003, pp. vi-ix).

Chapter 1

1. Kate Murphy, "Tuba Seller Toots His Own Horn As One of a Kind," *Miami Herald,* December 23, 2001, p. 8E.

2. <http://www.aircanada.ca/acfamily>.

3. Wendell R. Smith, "Product Differentiation and Market Segmentation As Alternative Marketing Strategies," *Journal of Marketing,* July 1956, pp. 3-8.

4. Art Weinstein, "Market Selection in Technology-Based Industry: Insights from Executives," in Rajan Varadarajan and Bernard Jaworski (eds.), *American Marketing Association Winter Educators' Conference Proceedings,* Newport Beach, CA, February 20-23, 1993, pp. 1-2.

5. Stavros P. Kalafatis and Vicki Cheston, "Normative Models and Practical Applications of Segmentation in Business Markets," *Industrial Marketing Management,* 26, 1997, pp. 519-530.

6. Stavros P. Kalafatis and Markos H. Tsogas, "Business Segmentation Bases: Congruence and Perceived Effectiveness," *Journal of Segmentation in Marketing,* 2(1), 1998, pp. 35-63.

7. Ali Kara and Erdener Kaynak, "Markets of a Single Customer: Exploiting Conceptual Developments in Market Segmentation," *European Journal of Marketing,* 31(11/12), 1997, pp. 873-895.

8. Christopher W. Hart, "Made to Order," *Marketing Management,* 5, Summer 1996, pp. 11-22.

9. Russell Haley, "Benefit Segmentation—Thoughts On Its Past and Its Future," *Journal of Segmentation in Marketing,* 3(1), 1999, p. 10.

10. Gregory Elliott and William J. Glynn, "A Portfolio-Based Approach to the Segmentation of Markets for Financial Services: Conceptual and Operational Issues," *Journal of Segmentation in Marketing,* 2(1), 1998, p. 81.

11. Tevfik Dalgic, "Niche Marketing Principles: Guerillas versus Gorillas," *Journal of Segmentation in Marketing*, 2(1), 1998, pp. 5-18.

12. Philip Kotler, *Marketing Management: The Millennium Edition* (Upper Saddle River, NJ: Prentice-Hall, 2000), p. 257.

13. Alex Salkever, "Finally, a Chance for Apple to Flourish," *Business Week Online*, January 18, 2002.

14. Reid Kanaley, "Expect Competition, Consolidation in Wireless Industry," *Miami Herald*, June 2, 2002, p. 6E.

Chapter 2

1. Jack Welch, *Jack: Straight from the Gut* (New York: Warner Books, 2001).

2. Sandra Vandermerwe, "How Increasing Value to Customers Improves Business Results," *Sloan Management Review*, Fall 2000, pp. 27-37.

3. Gary Hamel and C.K. Prahalad, "Seeing the Future First," *Fortune*, September 5, 1994, pp. 64-67, 70.

4. Sally Dibb, "Developing a Decision Tool for Identifying Operational and Attractive Segments," *Journal of Strategic Marketing*, 3, 1995, pp. 189-203.

5. Charles A. Rarick and John Vitton, "Mission Statements Make Cents," *Journal of Business Strategy*, 16, January-February 1995, pp. 11-12.

6. Darrell Rigby, *2000: Management Tools—Annual Survey of Senior Executives* (Boston: Bain and Company, June 2001), <http://bain.com/bainweb/about/insights/overview.asp>.

7. Joseph V. Quigley, "Vision: How Leaders Develop It, Share It, and Sustain It," *Business Horizons*, 37, September-October 1994, pp. 37-41.

8. William A. Sherdan, *Market Ownership: The Art and Science of Becoming #1* (New York: Amacom, 1994).

9. Philip Kotler, *Marketing Management: Analysis, Planning, Implementation, and Control*, Eighth Edition (Englewood Cliffs, NJ: Prentice-Hall, 1994).

10. Art Weinstein, "Redefining Technology Markets: Strategic Insights for Competitive Intelligence Professionals," *Society of Competitive Intelligence Professionals Annual International Conference Proceedings*, Arlington, VA, March 27-30, 1996, pp. 580-581.

11. Sara Q. Duffy, "Do Competitive Hospitals Really Adopt Technology Faster? An Analysis of the Influence of Alternative Relevant Market Definitions," *Eastern Economic Journal*, 18, Spring 1992, pp. 187-208.

12. Fred Wiersema, *Customer Intimacy: Pick Your Partners, Shape Your Culture, Win Together* (Santa Monica, CA: Knowledge Exchange, 1996).

13. Dan Thomas, "Strategy: What's Your Business," *Success*, July/August 1994, p. 13.

14. I thank Gary Korenjel for providing this example; personal communication, April 24, 1997.

Chapter 3

1. William D. Neal, "Shortcomings Plague the Industry," *Marketing News,* September 16, 2002, p. 37.

2. Art Weinstein, "Strategic Segmentation: A Planning Approach for Marketers," *Journal of Segmentation in Marketing,* 1(2), pp. 7-16.

3. Art Weinstein, "Ten-Point Program Customizes Segmentation Analysis," *Marketing News,* May 23, 1986, p. 22.

4. Patrick Butler, "Marketing Problems: From Analysis to Decision," *Marketing Intelligence and Planning,* 12(2), pp. 4-12.

5. Randall G. Chapman, "Problems Definition in Marketing Research," *The Journal of Consumer Marketing,* Spring 1989, pp. 51-59.

6. Stavros P. Kalafatis and Markos H. Tsogas, "Business Segmentation Bases: Congruence and Perceived Effectiveness," *Journal of Segmentation in Marketing,* 2(1), 1998, pp. 35-63.

7. <www.marketresearch.com>.

8. Skip Andrew, The National Center for Database Marketing.

9. *CorpTech Directory of Technology Companies,* <www.findmarketresearch. com>, June 1, 2000.

10. Art Weinstein, "Editorial Forum: Consumer Behavior, Research, and Segmentation," *Journal of Segmentation in Marketing,* 2(2), pp. 1-3.

15. Joel Raphael and I. Robert Parket, "The Need for Market Research in Executive Decision Making," *The Journal of Business and Industrial Marketing,* Winter/Spring 1991, pp. 15-21.

16. Paul Millier, "Intuition Can Help in Segmenting Industrial Markets," *Industrial Marketing Management,* 29, 2000, pp. 147-155.

Chapter 4

1. Yoram Wind and Richard Cardoza, "Industrial Market Segmentation," *Industrial Marketing Management,* 3, 1974, pp. 127-133.

2. Joel Garreau, *The Nine Nations of North America* (Boston: Houghton Mifflin, 1981).

3. Paige Bowers, "New South Finds Its Niche As a Midsize Contractor," *Atlanta Business Chronicle,* May 5, 2000.

4. Geocommunity Spatial News Release, "Largest Census-to-Census Population Increase in US History As Every State Gains, Census Bureau Reports," April 10, 2001, <www.geocomm.com>.

5. Sandra Yin, "New or Me Too?" *American Demographics,* September 2002, pp. 28-29.

6. Martha Farnsworth Riche, "Computer Mapping Takes Center Stage," *American Demographics,* June 1986, pp. 26-31.

7. Russell Abratt, "Market Segmentation Practices of Industrial Marketers," *Industrial Marketing Management,* 22, 1993, pp. 79-84.

8. Arthur M. Hughes, "How SIC Analysis Builds Sales," Database Marketing Institute, October 21, 2002, <http://www.dbmarketing.com/articles/Art158.htm>.

9. "4. What Are the Main Differences Between NAICS and SIC," *NAICS Association Newsletter,* February 4, 2002, pp. 2-3.

10. James W. McKie, "Market Definition and the SIC Approach," in Franklin M. Fisher (ed.), *Antitrust and Regulation: Essays in Memory of John J. McGowan* (Cambridge, MA: MIT Press, 1985), pp. 85-100.

11. "4. Free NAICS Code Searches," *NAICS Association Newsletter,* June 23, 2002, p. 6.

12. Art Weinstein, *Defining Your Market: Winning Strategies for High-Tech, Industrial, and Service Firms* (Binghamton, NY: The Haworth Press, 1998), pp. 67-69.

13. "Revision of the UK Standard Industrial Classification: 'Operation 2007'," <www.com-met2005.org.uk/SIC>.

Chapter 5

1. James C. Anderson and James A. Narus, "Partnering As a Focused Marketing Strategy," *California Management Review,* Spring 1991, pp. 95-113.

2. S. Greco, "Choose or Lose," *Inc.,* December 1998, pp. 57-66.

3. James D. Hlavacek and B.C. Ames, "Segmenting Industrial and High-Tech Markets," *Journal of Business Strategy,* Fall 1986, pp. 39-50.

4. For further information about the *Thomas Register* on CD-ROM contact the Thomas Publishing Company, New York, at (212) 695-0500.

5. Roland T. Rust, Valarie A. Zeithaml, and Katherine N. Lemon, *Driving Customer Equity: How Customer Value Is Reshaping Corporate Strategy* (New York: The Free Press, 2000), p. 191.

6. Dror Pockard, "Why CRM Is at a Fateful Crossroads," C/Net News.com, March 13, 2003.

7. S. Ram and Hyung-Shik Jung, "The Conceptualization and Measurement of Product Usage," *Journal of the Academy of Marketing Science,* Winter 1990, pp. 67-75.

8. Richard Koch, *The 80/20 Principle: The Secret of Achieving More with Less* (New York: Currency/Doubleday, 1998), pp. 65-68.

9. Malcolm McDonald and Beth Rogers, *Key Account Management* (Oxford, England: Butterworth-Heinemann, 1998).

10. This example emerged from a segmentation training program I conducted for the Novartis Generics division, Latin American region, May 29, 2001.

11. Art Weinstein, "Customer Retention: A Usage Segmentation and Customer Value Approach," *Journal of Targeting, Measurement and Analysis for Marketing,* 10(3), 2002. The case application used in this article was contributed by Robert Fast, Vice President of Fast Industries.

12. Steven J. Anderson and David W. Glascoff, "Index Number Calculation Procedures Involving Product Usage and Volume Segmentation Approaches to Market Segmentation," in L.M. Capella et al. (eds.), *Progress in Marketing Thought* (Mississippi State, MS: Southern Marketing Association, 1990), pp. 5-10.

13. Gerry Foster, "Bulls-Eye Marketing—The Key to Profitability," *Home Office Computing,* April 1991, pp. 24-25.

14. Charles W. Stryker, "The Sales Information System: Putting the System to Work," *Business Marketing,* July 1985, pp. 80, 82, 84.

Chapter 6

1. Art Weinstein and Rick Kates, "Defining and Segmenting Markets: A Presentation to Bayer's POC Worldwide Marketing Managers," Dedham, MA, May 13, 1999.

2. Sheelagh Matear and Richard Gray, "Benefit Segments in a Freight Transport Market," *European Journal of Marketing*, 29(12), 1995, pp. 43-58.

3. Rowland T. Moriarty and David J. Reibstein, "Benefit Segmentation in Industrial Markets," *Journal of Business Research*, December 1986, pp. 463-486.

4. Chatrathi P. Rao and Zhengyuan Wang, "Evaluating Alternative Segmentation Strategies in Standard Industrial Markets," *European Journal of Marketing*, 29(2), 1995, pp. 58-75.

5. Bill Merrilees, Rohan Bentley, and Ross Cameron, "Building Service Market Segmentation: The Case of Electrical and Mechanical Building Maintenance Services," *Journal of Business and Industrial Marketing*, 14(2), 1999, pp. 151-161.

6. Robert A. Garda, "How to Carve Niches for Growth in Industrial Markets," *Management Review*, August 1981, p. 19.

7. S. MacStravic, "Questions of Value in Health Care," *Marketing Health Services,* Winter 1997, pp. 50-53.

8. Donal Daly, "2002 Online Customer Respect Study of Fortune 100 Companies," <www.CustomerRespect.com>, October 25, 2002.

9. W. Chan Kim and Renee Mauborgne, "Value Innovation: The Strategic Logic of High Growth," *Harvard Business Review,* January/February 1997, pp. 102-112.

10. Dan Dunn, Jon Hulak, and D. Steven White, "Segmenting High-Tech Markets: A Value-Added Approach," *Marketing Intelligence and Planning*, 17(4), 1999, pp. 186-191.

11. Arun Sharma and Douglas M. Lambert, "Segmentation of Markets Based on Customer Service," *International Journal of Physical Distribution and Logistics Management,* 24(4), 1994, pp. 50-58.

12. Russell I. Haley, "Benefit Segmentation: A Decision-Oriented Research Tool," *Journal of Marketing,* July 1968, pp. 30-35.

13. Russell I. Haley, "Benefit Segments: Backwards and Forwards," *Journal of Advertising Research,* February/March 1984, pp. 19-25.

14. Russell I. Haley, *Developing Effective Communications Strategy: A Benefit Segmentation Approach* (New York: John Wiley and Sons, Inc., 1985).

15. Gary M. Mullet, "Benefit Segmentation in Practice," *Journal of Segmentation in Marketing,* 3(1), 1999, pp. 13-36.

16. Terri C. Albert, "Need-Based Segmentation and Customized Communication Strategies in a Complex-Commodity Industry: A Supply Chain Study," *Industrial Marketing Management,* 32, 2003, pp. 281-290.

17. V. Kasturi Rangan, Rowland T. Moriarty, and Gordon S. Swartz, "Segmenting Customers in Mature Industrial Markets," *Journal of Marketing,* 56, October 1992, pp. 72-82.

Chapter 7

1. Victoria L. Crittenden, William F. Crittenden, and Daniel F. Muzyka, "Segmenting the Business-to-Business Marketplace by Product Attributes and the Decision Process," *Journal of Strategic Marketing,* 10, 2002, pp. 3-20.

2. Thomas J. Peters and Robert H. Waterman Jr., *In Search of Excellence: Lessons from America's Best-Run Companies* (New York: Warner Books, 1982), pp. 156-199.

3. David T. DaCasto, "Segmenting Entrenched Markets by the Strength of the Supplier-Buyer Relationship Using a Transaction Cost Analysis Framework," *Journal of Segmentation in Marketing,* 1(1), 1997, pp. 95-107.

4. Richard E. Plank, "A Critical Review of Industrial Market Segmentation," *Industrial Marketing Management,* 14, May 1985, pp. 79-91.

5. Thomas V. Bonoma and Benson P. Shapiro, *Segmenting the Industrial Market* (Lexington, MA: Lexington Books, 1983).

6. Benson P. Shapiro and Thomas V. Bonoma, "How to Segment Industrial Markets," *Harvard Business Review,* May-June 1984, pp. 104-110.

7. Paul Christ, "Segmenting Reseller Markets: A Multi-Level Approach," *Journal of Segmentation in Marketing,* 1(1), 1997, pp. 75-94.

8. Dan Wascoe Jr., "Firm Recommends Catering to Travelers' Different Needs," *Minneapolis Star Tribune,* July 21, 1989, p. 1D.

9. Emanuel H. Demby, "Psychographics Revisited: The Birth of a Technique," *Marketing News,* January 2, 1989, p. 21.

10. Susan Dellinger, *Psycho-Geometrics* (Englewood Cliffs, NJ: Prentice-Hall, 1989).

11. Seymour H. Fine, "Buyer and Seller Psychographics in Industrial Purchase Decisions," *Journal of Business and Industrial Marketing,* Winter-Spring 1991, pp. 49-58.

12. Christopher B. Kuenne, "Segment-Based Marketing: From Dream to Reality," *Pharmaceutical Executive,* October 2000, pp. 54-68.

13. Agnes P. Olszewski et al., "Corporate Culture: A Strategy to Enter Entrenched Markets," *Journal of Business and Industrial Marketing,* 2(3), 1987, pp. 5-15.

14. Theo M.M. Verhallen, Ruud T. Frambach, and Jaideep Prabhu, "Strategy-Based Segmentation of Industrial Markets," *Industrial Marketing Management*, 27, 1998, pp. 305-313.

15. Karen Maru File and Russ Alan Prince, "A Psychographic Segmentation of Industrial Family Businesses," *Industrial Marketing Management*, 25, 1996, pp. 223-234.

16. Abbie Griffin, "PDMA Research on New Product Development Practices: Updating Trends and Benchmarking Best Practices," *Journal of Product Innovation Management*, 14, 1997, pp. 429-458.

17. SRI Consulting Business Intelligence, VALS Program Materials, <http://www.sric-bi.com/VALS/types.shtml>, December 31, 2002.

18. Steve Creedy, "Beware the Techno-Schizos," *The Australian*, March 25, 1997, p. 35.

19. Everett M. Rogers, *Diffusion of Innovations*, Third Edition (New York: The Free Press, 1983).

20. Eric von Hippel, *The Sources of Innovation* (New York: Oxford University Press, 1988).

21. Chris Easingwood and Anthony Koustelos, "Marketing High Technology: Preparation, Targeting, Positioning, Execution," *Business Horizons*, May/June 2000, pp. 27-34.

Chapter 8

1. Bruce D. Henderson, "The Origin of Strategy," *Harvard Business Review*, November- December 1989, pp. 139-143.

2. Larry Bossidy and Ram Charan, *Execution: The Discipline of Getting Things Done* (New York: Crown Business, 2002).

3. Lyndon Simkin and Sally Dibb, "Prioritising Target Markets," *Marketing Intelligence and Planning*, 16(7), 1998, pp. 407-417.

4. Malcolm McDonald and Ian Dunbar, *Market Segmentation: How to Do It, How to Profit from It*, Second Edition (London: Macmillan Business, 1998).

5. Steven A. Sinclair and Edward C. Stalling, "Perceptual Mapping: A Tool for Industrial Marketing: A Case Study," *The Journal of Business and Industrial Marketing*, Winter/Spring 1990, pp. 55-66.

6. Marvin Nesbit and Art Weinstein, "Positioning the High-Tech Product," in Harold E. Glass (ed.), *Handbook of Business Strategy Yearbook* (Boston: Warren, Gorham, and Lamont, Inc., 1989/1990), pp. 30-1–30-8.

7. Kirthi Kaltyanam and Shelby McIntyre, "The E-Marketing Mix: A Contribution of the E-Tailing Wars," *Journal of the Academy of Marketing Science*, 30(4), 2002, pp. 487-499.

8. David N. McArthur and Tom Griffin, "A Marketing Management View of Integrated Marketing Communications," *Journal of Advertising Research*, September/October 1997, pp. 19-26.

Chapter 9

1. John P. Workman, Jr., "Factors Contributing to Marketing's Limited Role in Product Development in Many High-Tech Firms," *Journal of Market Focused Management,* 2, 1998, pp. 257-279.

2. Mark Jenkins and Malcolm McDonald, "Market Segmentation: Organizational Archetypes and Research Agendas," *European Journal of Marketing,* 31(1), 1997, pp. 17-32.

3. Sally Dibb and Lyndon Simkin, "Market Segmentation: Diagnosing and Treating the Barriers," *Industrial Marketing Management,* 30, 2001, pp. 609-625.

4. Sally Dibb and Lyndon Simkin, "A Program for Implementing Market Segmentation," *Journal of Business and Industrial Marketing,* 12(1), 1997, pp. 51-65.

5. Hal W. Goetsch, "Conduct a Comprehensive Marketing Audit to Improve Marketing Planning," *Marketing News,* March 18, 1983, Section 2, p. 14.

6. Philip Kotler, William T. Gregor, and William H. Rodgers, III, "The Marketing Audit Comes of Age," *Sloan Management Review,* Winter 1989, pp. 49-62.

7. Yoram Wind, "Issues and Advances in Segmentation Research," *Journal of Marketing Research,* XV, August 1978, pp. 8-28.

8. Don E. Schultz, "Behavior Changes: Do Your Segments?" *Marketing News,* July 22, 2002, pp. 5-6.

9. Allen C. Stines, telephone conversation, February 20, 2003.

10. Susanne Goller, Annik Hogg, and Stavros Kalafatis, "A New Research Agenda for Business Segmentation," *European Journal of Marketing,* 36(1/2), 2002, pp. 252-271.

11. Per Vagn Freytag and Ann Hojbjerg Clarke, "Business to Business Market Segmentation," *Industrial Marketing Management,* 30, 2001, pp. 473-486.

Index

Page numbers followed by the letter "f" indicate figures; those followed by the letter "t" indicate tables

Small firms, 8, 9, 12, 70, 71, 72-73,
    123, 183, 184
Smith, Wendell, 4, 167
Soft targets, 116
Sony, 5
Sophistication (of segmentation), 51,
    158, 168-169
South Africa, 71
Southwest Airlines, 25
Speed of delivery, 9
Sportmed, 219-223
SQIP (service, quality, image, and
    price), 101-102
SRC, 70
SRI International, 125-127
St. Joe Company, 23t
Standardized market area measures,
    64-65
Static versus dynamic segmentation,
    169
Statistical software, 49
Steel market examples, 32t, 108, 111t,
    114
Strategic
    groups, 203, 205, 207, 208
    marketing, 123, 133-154, 158-165,
        204-207
    types, 123
Strengths and weaknesses, 91, 142t
Strategy Consulting, Inc., 87
Subsegmentation, 19
Substitute industries, 203, 204-205,
    207, 208
Switching vendors, 116
Syndicated sources, 43, 124-127
Synergy, 143

Target, retail store, 113
Target market
    concept, 27f, 29-30, 33, 137
    examples, 3, 6, 14, 29, 32t, 57-58,
        63, 74, 99-100, 103-104, 108,
        121-123, 124, 126, 127-129,
        154t, 178-179, 223

Target market (continued)
    profile, 98f, 154t, 179
    strategy, 133-154
    strategy worksheet, 143, 144
Target population measurement units,
    38
Technical requirements/specifications,
    9, 139, 140f
Technographics, 127
Technology, 116, 118f, 123, 127-129,
    220-221
Telecommunications market, 103-104,
    123
Texas Instruments, 169
Thinking outside of the box, 115, 169
Thomas Register of American
    Manufacturers, 83
Three-stage approach, 9
TIGER (Topologically Integrated
    Geographic Encoding and
    Referencing), 68-69
Time, 203, 206, 207, 208
Trends, 120, 165, 167-169
Trial and error, 52
Toshiba, 5
Tsogas, Markos, 9, 40t
Tuba Exchange, 3
Two-stage approach, 9, 62, 116
Typical users, 84

Uncertainty, 49
Underanalysis, 34
Undifferentiation, 7, 8, 12t, 15
Uniform supply company example, 74
Universities (as a resource), 52
Unobservable characteristics, 123
Unordered segmentation, 116
Unprofitable customers, 84
Untapped market, 27f, 29, 32t
Upjohn, 211
Urgency of order, 116, 118f
Usage
    analysis, 81-95
    assessment, 91-94